Curious Myths
of the
Middle Ages

THE REV. SABINE BARING-GOULD

Curious Myths
of the
Middle Ages

EDITED AND WITH AN INTRODUCTION
BY EDWARD HARDY

CRESCENT BOOKS
NEW YORK

This 1987 Edition published by Cresent Books
distributed by Crown Publishers, Inc.,
225 Park Avenue South, New York 10003

ISBN 0 517 63992 0

h   g   j   e   d   c   b   a

Printed and bound in Great Britain by
Mackays of Chatham, Kent.

Too much curiosity lost Paradise.

APHRA BEHN *The Lucky Chance*

Contents

A Note on the Illustrations

THE woodcuts used to illustrate *Curious Myths of the Middle Ages* are all the work of Albrecht Dürer. They are as follows: CHAPTER ONE A title cut from the *Works* of Jean Charlier de Gerson, *c.* 1489. CHAPTER TWO From Sebastian Brant's *Narrenschiff*, Basle, 1494-5. CHAPTER THREE *Ritter von Turn*, Basle, 1493. CHAPTER FOUR *Ritter von Turn*. CHAPTER FIVE A Nuremberg prayer-book, *c.* 1503. CHAPTER SIX Sebastian Brant from *Varia Carmina von Sebastian Brant*, 1498. CHAPTER SEVEN *Narrenschiff*. CHAPTER EIGHT From the title page of *Oratio Cassandre Venete*, *c.* 1488. CHAPTER NINE Main-title page of *Messahalah, De Scientia motus orbis*, Nuremberg, 1504. CHAPTER TEN *Narrenschiff*. CHAPTER ELEVEN *Narrenschiff*. CHAPTER TWELVE *Ritter von Turn*. CHAPTER THIRTEEN *Narrenschiff*. CHAPTER FOURTEEN *Narrenschiff*. CHAPTER FIFTEEN The Albertina Passion series, *c.* 1500. CHAPTER SIXTEEN *Narrenschiff*. CHAPTER SEVENTEEN *Ritter von Turn*. CHAPTER EIGHTEEN From *Prima Pars Doctrinalis*, Nuremberg, 1491. CHAPTER NINETEEN From a series illustrating the *Comedies* of Terence, *c.* 1496. CHAPTER TWENTY *Ritter von Turn*. CHAPTER TWENTY-ONE *Ritter von Turn*. CHAPTER TWENTY-TWO *Ritter von Turn*. CHAPTER TWENTY-THREE *Ritter von Turn*. CHAPTER TWENTY-FOUR *Ritter von Turn*.

All of Dürer's extant works have been collected by Dr. Willi Kurth in *The Complete Woodcuts of Albrecht Dürer* (London, 1927, and many times reprinted). The most perceptive study of Dürer and his times is still Erwin Panofsky's *The Life and Art of Albrecht Dürer* (London and New York, 1955).   A.F.

Introduction

SABINE BARING-GOULD was born at Exeter on 28 January 1834, the eldest son of a country gentleman, with estates at Lew Trenchard in Devon, and of an admiral's daughter. He was privately educated, mainly abroad, on account of his ill-health, an experience which was successful from every aspect since he lived to his ninetieth year and became a good linguist, particularly in German, the language in which the best nineteenth-century research was published. At the age of eighteen he went to Clare College, Cambridge, and left with a degree after three years to take up a career as a schoolmaster. After a short spell at the choir school of St Barnabas, Pimlico, he went on to a seven-year stint at Hurstpierpoint College. After this, at the age of thirty, he was ordained as a priest of the Church of England and began his clerical career as curate of Horbury, Yorkshire, an area not particularly marked for its Anglicanism nor, for that matter, for its religion, but where he served a useful apprenticeship in the observation of dissenters, drunkenness and demonism – some of his observations on the Wesleyan methodists and the pagan folk-lore which he encountered in Yorkshire occur in this book. In 1871, when he was 37, he became rector of East Mersey (now East Mersea) in Essex. Next year his father died and he inherited the family estates. This legacy included the patronage of the local church living, but he had to wait nine years more for the incumbent to die. He then presented himself to the family living, went home for good, and continued as rector of Lew Trenchard, Devon, for well over forty years more.

Baring-Gould began writing books from the time he became a schoolmaster in 1857. He married a local girl after he arrived in Yorkshire, and he was so prolific that he produced in his lifetime 159 books and fourteen children. He was a good researcher, though he was said to lack finesse in the details of criticism. He himself considered that his most important work was *The Origin and Development of Religious Belief*, which was published in two volumes in 1869 and 1870 while he was still in Yorkshire. He went on to write *The Lives of the Saints* in fifteen volumes published between 1872 and 1877, *The Lives of the British Saints* in 1907 and his heavily criticised *History of the Evangelical Revival* in 1920. Besides many volumes of sermons he published a number of hymns, of which the best-known is 'Onward, Christian Soldiers' – a sentiment very characteristic of him as may be gathered from his chapter on Saint George in the present book.

He had a very deep interest in legend and folk-lore which was strengthened by his quick facility both in languages and research. After writing *A Book of Were-Wolves* in 1865 during his first year in Yorkshire he went rapidly on to complete the present volume, *Curious Myths of the Middle Ages*, published in 1866, highly successful and often reprinted. In later years he published a number of books on the West Country, concerning himself with its folk-lore and history as well as its natural beauty: *A Book of the West*, 1899, is only one of many. His most valuable work in this sphere was to catch the words of the old folk-songs before the singers died away for ever, and he published *Collected Folk-songs and Ballads of Devon and Cornwall in* 1890 and *Songs of the West* in 1905. He did not confine himself to England, but travelled widely on the Continent and wrote four travel-books about France. He wrote many novels, of which the first, *Mehalah*, 1880, was compared by Swinburne with *Wuthering Heights*. In his last years he wrote two books of reminiscences which were published in 1923 and 1925, on either side of his death, 2 January 1924.

Sabine Baring-Gould was a man of lively observation and with almost a magpie-store of memory who, like Sherlock Holmes, darted apparently intuitively to the solution of a problem, though perhaps not always so accurately as the man from Baker Street. His work on the myths of the middle ages has never, in spite of massive modern research, been bettered for middlebrow presentation. In editing his massive original volume I have ruthlessly abandoned the farther shores of his research, but the enthusiast should still consult it for reference to all the principal authorities in the field up to the mid-nineteenth century.

EDWARD HARDY

Feast of St Pancras 1977

Curious Myths
of the
Middle Ages

1.

The Wandering Jew

THERE ARE MANY accounts in ancient chronicles of a restless
wanderer, often said to have been a Jewish shoemaker who
refused to allow Jesus to rest for a moment on his doorstep as he
carried his cross to the place of crucifixion, who was doomed to walk
the world for ever and was barred even from suicide. Because the
names and circumstances vary in almost every account, historians
nowadays claim no accuracy for the events. They persist as a constant myth emphasising the tragedy, and often the majesty, of an
individual who has been given an immortality he did not seek,
doomed to wander over the face of the earth, seeking rest and finding
none.

The earliest surviving mention of the Wandering Jew occurs in the
book of the chronicles of the Abbey of St Albans, the *Chronica Majora*
which was copied and continued by Matthew Paris. Matthew records
that in the year 1228 'a certain Archbishop of Armenia Major came
on a pilgrimage to England to see the relics of the saints, and to visit
the sacred places in the kingdom, as he had done in others. He also
produced letters of recommendation from his Holiness the Pope to
the leaders of religious communities and to the prelates of the churches, in which they were enjoined to receive and entertain him with
due reverence and honour. On his arrival, he went to St Albans,
where he was received with all respect by the abbot and the monks.
At this place, being fatigued with his journey, he remained some days

to rest himself and his followers. A conversation was commenced between him and the inhabitants of the convent, by means of their interpreters, during which he made many enquiries concerning the religion and religious observances of this country, and related many strange things concerning Eastern countries. In the course of the conversation he was asked whether he had ever seen or heard anything of Joseph, a man of whom there was much talk in the world, who, when our Lord suffered, was present and spoke to him, and who is still alive, in evidence of the Christian faith. A knight in the archbishop's retinue replied, speaking French:

My lord well knows that man, and a little before he took his way to the western countries, the said Joseph ate at the table of my lord the Archbishop of Armenia, who had previously often seen and held converse with him.

The knight was then asked about what had passed between Christ and the said Joseph, to which he replied:

At the time of the suffering of Jesus Christ, he was seized by the Jews and led into the hall of judgment before Pilate, the governor, that he might be judged by him on the accusation of the Jews; and Pilate, finding no cause for adjudging him to death, said to them 'Take him and judge him according to your law.' The shouts of the Jews, however, increasing, he at their request released unto them Barabbas, and delivered Jesus to them to be crucified. When, therefore, the Jews were dragging Jesus forth and he had reached the door, Cartaphilus, a porter of the hall in Pilate's service, as Jesus was going out of the door, imperiously struck him on the back with his hand and said in mockery 'Go quicker, Jesus, go quicker. Why do you loiter?' Jesus, looking back on him with a severe countenance, said to him 'I am going, and you will wait till I return.'

And according as our Lord said, this Cartaphilus is still awaiting his return. At the time of our Lord's suffering he was thirty years old, and when he attains the age of a hundred years he always returns to the same age as he was when our Lord suffered. After Christ's death, when the Catholic faith gained ground, this Cartaphilus was baptized by Ananias (who also baptized the apostle Paul), and was called Joseph. He often dwells in both divisions of Armenia and other Eastern countries, passing his time amidst the bishops and other prelates of the Church. He is a man of holy conversation, and religious; a man of few words, and circumspect in his behaviour; for he does not speak at all unless when questioned by the bishops and religious men; and then he tells of the events of old times, and of the incidents which occurred at the suffering and resurrection of our Lord, and of the witnesses of the resurrection – namely, those who rose with Christ and went into the holy city and appeared unto men. He also tells of the creed of the apostles, and of their separation and preaching. And all this he relates without smiling or levity of conversation, as one who is well practised in sorrow and the fear of God, always looking forward with fear to the coming of Jesus Christ, lest at the Last Judgment he should find Christ in anger whom, when he was on his way to death, he had provoked to just vengeance. Numbers came to him from different parts of the world, enjoying his society and conversation; and to them, if they are men of authority, he explains all doubts on the matters on which he is questioned. He refuses all gifts that are offered to him, being content with slight food and clothing. He places his hope of salvation on the fact that he sinned through ignorance, for the Lord when suffering prayed for his enemies in these words: 'Father, forgive them, for they know not what they do.'

Shortly after the date of the chronicle of Matthew Paris, Philip Mouskes, afterwards Bishop of Tournay, wrote a rhymed chronicle in 1242 which contains a similar account of the Jew derived from the same Armenian prelate, mentioning that this man had visited the shrine of St Thomas of Canterbury (who had been martyred in 1170) and had then made the great pilgrimage to the church of St James of Compostella, and had come back east to Cologne to see the heads of the Three Kings.

There is a gap in the surviving written references to the Wandering Jew which extends for over 250 years after Philip Mouskes, but it seems that this is through the destruction of manuscripts rather than the fading of the legend, for the character of the Wandering Jew is referred to quite casually in a Bohemian story of 1505 about a seventy-year-old traveller who assisted in the recovery of some buried treasure. In completely different surroundings, an Arab manuscript mentions him a few years later as expounding the Christian faith to the leader of a Moslem regiment of cavalry.

A circumstantial and corroborated account of his appearance in Hamburg in 1547 was given by Paul von Eitzen, a doctor of the holy scriptures who afterwards became Bishop of Schleswig, where he died in 1598 aged 76. The biography of the bishop was written by Greve, and the earliest surviving copy is now an edition printed in Hamburg in 1744.

Dr von Eitzen related that when he was young, having studied at Wittemberg, he returned home to his parents in Hamburg in the winter of the year 1547. On the following Sunday, in church, he observed a tall man with his hair hanging over his shoulders, standing barefoot during the sermon, over against the pulpit, listening with the deepest attention to the discourse. Whenever the name of Jesus was mentioned he bowed himself profoundly and humbly with sighs and beating of the breast. He had no other clothing in the bitter cold of the winter except a pair of hose which were in tatters about his feet and a coat with a girdle which reached to his feet. His general appearance was that of a man of fifty years. And many people, some of high degree and title, have seen this same man in England, France, Italy, Hungary, Persia, Spain, Poland, Moscow, Lapland, Sweden, Denmark, Scotland and other places.

Every one wondered over the man. After the sermon the doctor inquired diligently where the stranger was to be found, and when he had sought him out he enquired of him privately whence he came, and how long that winter he had been in the place. Thereupon he replied modestly that he was a Jew by birth, a native of Jerusalem, by name Ahasverus, by trade a shoemaker. He had been present at the crucifixion of Christ, and had lived ever since, travelling through various lands and cities, the which he substantiated by accounts he gave. He related also the circumstances of Christ's tranference from Pilate to Herod, and the final crucifixion, together with other details not recorded by the evangelists and the historians. He gave accounts of the changes of government in many countries, especially of the East, through several centuries, and moreover he detailed the labours and deaths of the holy apostles of Christ most circumstantially.

Now when Dr von Eitzen heard this with profound astonishment, on account of its incredible novelty, he inquired further, in order that he might obtain more accurate information. Then the man answered that he had lived in Jerusalem at the time of the crucifixion of Christ, whom he had regarded as a deceiver of the people and a heretic. He had seen him with his own eyes and had done his best, along with others, to bring this deceiver, as he regarded him, to justice and to have him put out of the way. When the sentence had been pronounced by Pilate, Christ was about to be dragged past his house. Then he ran home and called his household to have a look at Christ and see what sort of a person he was.

This having been done, he had his little child on his arm, and was standing in his doorway to have a sight of the Lord Jesus Christ.

As Christ was led by, bowed under the weight of the heavy cross, he tried to rest a little, and stood still a moment. But the shoemaker, in zeal and rage, and for the sake of obtaining credit among the other Jews, drove the Lord Christ forward and told him to hasten on his way. Jesus, obeying, looked at him and said: "I shall stand and rest, but thou shalt go till the last day." At these words the man set down the child and, unable to remain where he was, he followed Christ and saw how cruelly he was crucified, how he suffered, how he died. As soon as this had taken place it came upon him suddenly that he could no more return to Jerusalem, nor see again his wife and child, but must go forth into foreign lands, one after another, like a mournful pilgrim. When, years after, he returned to Jerusalem, he found it ruined and utterly razed, so that not one stone was left standing on another. He could not recognize former localities.

He believes that it is God's purpose in thus driving him about in miserable life and preserving him undying, to present him before the Jews at the end as a living token, so that the godless and unbelieving may remember the death of Christ and be turned to repentance. For his part he would well rejoice were God in heaven to release him from this vale of tears.

After this conversation, Doctor Paul von Eitzen, along with the rector of the school at Hamburg, who was well read in history, and a traveller, questioned him about events which had taken place in the East since the death of Christ, and he was able to give them much information on many matters, so that it was impossible not to be convinced of the truth of his story, and to see that what seems impossible with men is, after all, possible with God.

Since the Jew has had his life extended he has become silent and reserved, and only answers direct questions. When invited to become anyone's guest, he eats little and drinks in great moderation, then hurries on, never remaining long in one place. When at Hamburg, Dantzig and elsewhere money has been offered to him he never took more than two schillings [about two new pence] and at once distributed it to the poor, as token that he needed no money, for God would provide for him, as he rued the sins he had committed in ignorance.

During the period of his stay in Hamburg and Dantzig he was never seen to laugh. In whatever land he travelled he spoke its language, and when he spoke Saxon it was like a native Saxon. Many people came from different places to Hamburg and Dantzig in order to see and hear this man, and were convinced that the providence of God was exercised in this individual in a very remarkable manner. He gladly listened to God's word, or heard it spoken of always with great gravity and compunction, and he ever reverenced with sighs the pronunciation of the name of God or of Jesus Christ, and could not endure to hear curses, but when ever he heard any one swear by God's death or pains, he waxed indignant and exclaimed with vehemence and with sighs: "Wretched man and miserable creature thus to misuse the name of the Lord thy God and his bitter sufferings and passion. Hadst thou seen, as I have, how heavy and bitter were the pangs and wounds of thy Lord, endured for thee and for me, thou wouldest rather undergo great pain thyself than thus take his sacred name in vain!"

Such is the account given to me by Doctor Paul von Eitzen, with many circumstantial proofs, and corroborated by certain of my own old acquaintances who saw this same individual with their eyes in Hamburg.

In the year 1575 the Secretary Christopher Klause and Master Jacob von Holstein, legates to the Court of Spain, and afterwards sent into the Netherlands to pay the soldiers serving his Majesty in that country, related on their return home to Schleswig, and confirmed with solemn oaths, that they had come across the same mysterious individual at Madrid in Spain, in appearance, manner of life, habits, clothing, just the same as he had appeared at Hamburg. They said that they had spoken with him, and that many people of all classes had conversed with him, and found him to speak good Spanish. In the year 1590, in December, a reliable person wrote from Brunswick to Strasburg that the same mentioned strange person had been seen alive at Vienna in Austria, and that he had started for Poland and Dantzig; and that he purposed going on to Moscow. This Ahasverus was at Lubeck in 1601, also about the same date in Revel in Livonia, and in Cracow in Poland. In Moscow he was seen of many and spoken to by many.

What thoughtful God-fearing persons are to think of the said person is their option. God's works are wondrous and past finding out, and are manifested day by day, only to be revealed in full at the last great day of account.

This account, quoted in the biography of Bishop von Eitzen, was in the form of an affidavit drawn up at Revel [*at that time occupied by Sweden, later part of Russia, later capital of Estonia, now the Russian fortified seaport Tallinn*] which was drawn up on the 1 August 1613 and was signed before witnesses by Chrysostomus Duduloeus of Westphalia.

The Wandering Jew was also reported by Henricus Bangert to have been seen in Lubeck in 1603, and by Rudolf Botoreus to have been in Paris in 1604. Other reports placed him in Hamburg again in 1633 and in Brussels in 1640, and Leipzig in 1642. There is an account which may be read in full in Peck's *History of Stamford* that he knocked at the door of the ailing Samuel Wallis of Stamford, Lincolnshire 'upon Whitsunday in the year of our Lord 1658, about six of the clock, just after evensong,' and gave the consumptive Wallis medical advice, but there was no particular reference to his having been present at the crucifixion of Christ. At the end of that century a man who called himself the Wandering Jew appeared in England and was taken up frivolously by the nobility 'who paid him as they might a juggler'. He declared that he had been an officer of the Sanhedrim and that he had struck Christ as he was leaving the judgment-hall of Pilate. He remembered all the apostles and described their personal appearance, their clothes and their peculiarities. He spoke many languages, claimed the power of healing the sick, and asserted that he had travelled nearly all over the world. Those who heard him were perplexed by his familiarity with foreign tongues and places. Oxford and Cambridge sent professors to question him. An English nobleman conversed with him in Arabic and questioned him about Mahomet. The man said he had known Mahomet's father at Ormuz, that he believed Mahomet was an intelligent man, and that once when he had heard the prophet deny that Christ was crucified, he himself answered abruptly that he was a witness to the truth of that event. He also said that he had been in Rome when Nero set it on fire, and that he had known Saladin, Tamerlane and many other conquerors. In addition he gave minute details of the Crusades. This man left London, was reported in Denmark and Sweden, and then passed out of the annals.

Men who were either impostors claiming to be the Wandering Jew, or lunatics who actually believed they were this unhappy man, appeared in England in 1818, 1824 and 1830 according to an analysis in the *Athenaeum* of 3 November 1866. No later firm reports of him have occurred.

Clearly the accounts are without sufficient historical authenticity to be regarded as anything but myth. But no myth is itself without foundation, even as a symbol of a poetic truth. The story has been taken as a crystallisation of the odyssey of the descendants of Cain, wandering over the earth with the brand of a brother's blood as their curse, or of the Gipsies, of whom it has been said that they have lived under a similar curse because they refused shelter to the Virgin and Child on their flight into Egypt. The story has also been linked with the legend of the Wild Huntsman in the Harz mountains, a great cradle of German folklore. One version there is that the Wild Huntsman is a Jew who refused to allow Jesus to take a drink from his well but contemptuously pointed out to him the hoof-print of a horse in which a little water had collected. In the mountains of France the sudden roar of a gale at night is identified as the passing of the Everlasting Jew. A Swiss story says that he was seen on the Matterberg, below the Matterhorn, contemplating the scene with mingled sorrow and wonder. Once before he had stood on that hill, and then it was the site of a flourishing city. But now it is covered with gentian and wild pinks. He will revisit that hill once more, and that will be on the eve of Judgment.

2.

Prester John

At about the middle of the twelfth century a rumour circulated through Europe that there reigned in Asia a powerful Christian emperor, Presbyter Johannes. In a bloody fight he had broken the power of the Mohammedans and was ready to come to the assistance of the Crusaders. The West was enduring a time of military defeat against the dangerous Arab invasion, and Pope Alexander III determined at once to form an alliance with this mysterious person. On 27 September 1177 he wrote him a letter which he entrusted to his physician, Philip, to deliver in person. Philip started on his embassy, but never returned.

The Mongol hordes of Gengis Khan now made a massed invasion of Europe and swept over Russia, Poland, Hungary and east Germany before they were halted at the battle of Liegnitz. Pope Innocent IV determined to convert these barbarians and sent a number of Dominican and Franciscan missionaries among them. Embassies of peace passed between the Pope, the King of France, and the Mogul Khan. The result of these communications with the East was that travellers learned how false were the prevalent notions of a mighty Christian kingdom existing in central Asia. Popular belief therefore changed, and transferred the monarchy of the famous Priest-King to central Africa, to Abyssinia, where there was indeed some basis for that belief. But some men of the world, among whom was Marco Polo, while acknowledging the existence of a Christian monarch in

Abyssinia, still stoutly maintained that the Prester John of popular belief reigned in splendour somewhere in the dim Orient.

The first known report of the monarchy of Prester John occurs in a chronicle of Otto of Freisingen written in the mid-twelfth century which states that in 1145 the Catholic Bishop of Cabala visited Europe to lay certain complaints before the Pope, and among other reports

... he stated that a few years ago a certain King and Priest called John, who lives on the further side of Persia and Armenia in the remote East, and who, with all his people, were Christians, although belonging to the Nestorian Church, had overcome the royal brothers Samiardi, kings of the Medes and Persians, and had captured Ecbatana, their capital and residence ... The said John was hastening to the assistance of the Church in Jerusalem, but his army, on reaching the Tigris, was hindered from passing through a deficiency of boats, and he directed his march north-wards, since he had heard that the river was there covered with ice. In that place he had waited many years, expecting severe cold, but the winters having proved unpropitious, and the severity of the climate having carried off many soldiers, he had been forced to retreat to his own land.

This king belongs to the family of the Magi mentioned in the gospels, and he rules over the very people formerly governed by the Magi. More-over, his fame and his wealth is so great that he uses an emerald sceptre only. Excited by the example of his ancestors, who came to worship Christ in his cradle, he had proposed to go to Jerusalem, but had been impeded by the above-mentioned causes.

There were other contemporary reports of Prester John. Maimo-nides (1135-1204) referred to 'a strange people in the lands of Babel and Teman, governed by a Christian chief, Preste-Cuan by name.' Benjamin of Tudela, who died in 1173 after 24 years of travel in the East, referred to a fabulous Jewish king who reigned in the utmost splendour over a realm inhabited by Jews alone somewhere in the middle of a vast desert.

But even more remarkable was the reproduction in the chronicle of Albericus Trium Fontium of a letter said to have been written in 1165 by Prester John himself to Manuel of Comnenus, Emperor of Constantinople (1143-1180). Similar letters were also said to have been sent to Frederic the Roman Emperor, Pope Alexander III, Louis VII of France and to the King of Portugal, and alleged excerpts from it were put into rhyme and sung all over Europe by minstrels and trouvères.

The text of the missive reported to have been sent by Prester John to the Emperor of Constantinople is perhaps the most grandiloquent despatch ever entrusted to any diplomatic bag. It is the source of all the wondrous tales of the Asian King which endured for five centuries well past Shakespeare's time. It reads, in part:

John, Priest by the almighty power of God and the might of our Lord Jesus Christ, King of Kings and Lord of Lords, to his friend Emanuel, Prince of Constantinople, wishing him health, prosperity, and the continuance of divine favour.

Our Majesty has been informed that you hold our Excellency in love and that the report of our greatness has reached you. Moreover we have heard through our treasurer that you have been pleased to send to us some objects of art and interest, that our Exaltedness might be gratified thereby.

Being human, I receive it in good part, and we have ordered our treasurer to send you some of our articles in return.

Now we desire to be made certain that you hold the right faith, and in all things cleave to Jesus Christ our Lord, for we have heard that your court regard you as a god, though we know that you are mortal, and subject to human infirmities . . .

Should you desire to learn the greatness and excellency of our Exaltedness and of the land subject to our sceptre, then hear and believe: I, Presbyter Johannes, the Lord of Lords, surpass all under heaven in virtue, in riches and in power. Seventy-two kings pay us tribute . . . In the three Indies our Magnificence rules, and our land extends beyond India, where rests the body of the holy apostle Thomas; it reaches towards the sunrise over the wastes, and it trends towards deserted Babylon near the tower of Babel. Seventy-two provinces, of which only a few are Christian, serve us. Each has its own king, but all are tributary to us.

Our land is the home of elephants, dromedaries, camels, crocodiles, wild asses, white and red lions, white bears, white merles, crickets, griffins, tigers, lamias, hyaenas, wild horses, wild oxen and wild men, men with horns, one-eyed men, men with eyes before and behind, centaurs, fauns, satyrs, pygmies, forty-ell high giants, Cyclopses, and similar women; it is the home, too, of the phoenix, and of nearly all living animals. We have some people subject to us who feed on the flesh of men and of prematurely born animals, and who never fear death. When any of these people die, their friends and relations eat him ravenously, for they regard it as a main duty to munch human flesh. Their names are Gog and Magog [*and ten others*]. These and similar nations were shut in behind lofty mountains by Alexander the Great, towards the North. We lead them at our pleasure against our foes, and neither man nor beast is left undevoured, if our Majesty gives the requisite permission. And when all our foes are eaten, then we return with our hosts [*armies*] home again. These accursed fifteen nations will burst forth from the four quarters of the earth at the end of the world, in the times of Antichrist, and overrun all the abodes of the Saints as well as the great city Rome – which, by the way, we are prepared to give to our un-born son, along with all Italy, Germany, the two Gauls, Britain and Scotland. We shall also give him Spain and all the land as far as the icy sea. The nations to which I have alluded, according to the words of the prophet, shall not stand in the judgment on account of their offensive practices, but will be consumed to ashes by a fire which will fall on them from heaven.

Our land streams with honey and is overflowing with milk. In our re-gion grows no poisonous herb, nor does a querulous frog ever croak in it, nor does the serpent glide among the grass, nor can any poisonous animals exist in it or injure any one.

Among the heathen, flows through a certain province the river Indus; encircling Paradise, it spreads its arms in manifold windings through the entire province. Here are found the emeralds, sapphires, carbuncles, topazes, chrysolites, onyxes, beryls, sardius, and other costly stones. Here grows the plant Assidos, which, when worn by any one, protects him from the evil spirit, forcing it to state its business and name; consequently the foul spirits keep out of the way there. In a certain land subject to us pepper of all kinds is gathered and is exchanged for corn and bread, leather and cloth . . . At the foot of Mount Olympus bubbles up a spring which changes its flavour hour by hour, night and day, and the spring is scarcely three days' journey from Paradise, out of which Adam was driven. If any one has tasted thrice of that fountain, from that day he will feel no fatigue, but will as long as he lives be as a man of thirty years. Here are found the small stones called Nudiosi, which, if borne about the body, prevent the sight from waxing feeble and restore it where it is lost. The more the stone is looked at the keener becomes the sight. In our territory is a certain waterless sea, consisting of tumbling billows of sand never at rest. None have crossed this sea; it lacks water altogether, yet fish are cast up upon the beach, very tasty, and the like are nowhere else to be seen. Three days' journey from this sea are mountains from which rolls down a stony water-less river which opens into the sandy sea. As soon as the stream reaches the sea its stones vanish in it and are never seen again. As long as the river is in motion it cannot be crossed; only four days a week is it possible to traverse it. Between the sandy sea and the said mountains, in a certain plain is a fountain of singular virtue, which purges Christians and would-be Chris-tians from all transgressions. The water stands four inches high in a hollow stone shaped like a mussel-shell. Two saintly old men watch by it, and ask the comers whether they are Christians, or about to become Christians, and then whether they desire healing with all their heart. If they have answered well they are bidden to lay aside their clothes and to step into the mussel. If what they said be true, then the water begins to rise and gush over their heads; thrice does the water thus lift itself and every one who has entered the mussel leaves it cured of every complaint.

Near the wilderness trickles between barren mountains a subterranean rill, which can only by chance be reached, for only occasionally the earth gapes, and he who would descend must do it with precipitation ere the earth closes again. All that is gathered under the ground there is gem and precious stone. The brook pours into another river, and the inhabitants of the neighbourhood obtain thence abundance of precious stones. Yet they never venture to sell them without first having offered them to us for our private use: should we decline them, they are at liberty to dispose of them to strangers. Boys there are trained to remain three or four days under water, diving after the stones.

Beyond the stone river are the ten tribes of the Jews, which, though subject to their own kings, are for all that our slaves and tributary to our Majesty. In one of our lands hight [*called*] Zone, are worms [*dragons*] called in our tongue Salamanders. These worms can only live in fire, and they build cocoons like silkworms, which are unwound by the ladies of our palace and spun into cloth and dresses, which are worn by our Exaltedness. These dresses in order to be cleaned and washed are cast into flames . . .

When we go to war we have fourteen golden and bejewelled crosses borne before us instead of banners; each of these crosses is followed by 10,000 horsemen and 100,000 foot soldiers fully armed, without reckoning those in charge of the luggage and provision.

When we ride abroad plainly, we have a wooden, unadorned cross, without gold or gem about it, borne before us in order that we may meditate on the sufferings of our Lord Jesus Christ; also a golden bowl filled with earth, to remind us of that whence we sprang and that to which we must return; but besides these there is borne a silver bowl full of gold as a token that we are the Lord of Lords.

All riches such as are upon the world our Magnificence possesses in superabundance. With us no one lies, for he who speaks a lie is thenceforth regarded as dead – he is no more thought of or honoured by us. No vice is tolerated by us. Every year we undertake a pilgrimage, with retinue of war, to the body of the holy prophet Daniel, which is near the desolated site of Babylon. In our realm fishes are caught, the blood of which dyes purple. The Amazons and Brahmins are subject to us. The palace in which our Supereminency resides is built after the pattern of the castle built by the apostle Thomas for the Indian king Gundoforus. [*There follows a flamboyant description of the ebony, crystal, gold, amethyst, ivory and onyx with which this palace is constructed with, at the end of each gable,* two golden apples, in each of which are two carbuncles, so that the gold may shine by day and the carbuncles by night.] Before our palace stands a mirror, the ascent to which consists of five and twenty steps of porphyry and serpentine. It is adorned with gems and guarded night and day by three thousand armed men. We look therein and behold all that is taking place in every province and region subject to our sceptre.

Seven kings wait upon us monthly, in turn, with sixty-two dukes and two hundred and fifty-six counts and marquises: and twelve archbishops sit at table with us on our right and twenty bishops on the left, besides the patriarch of St Thomas, the Sarmatian Protopope, and the Archpope of Susa . . . Our lord high steward is an archbishop and king, our chamberlain a bishop and king, our marshal a king and abbot . . .

The letter goes on to describe the church in which Prester John worships and the precious stones, with their special virtues, with which it is constructed. The whole tone of the despatch is disparaging to Western Christendom, and it was to this depreciation that Pope Alexander principally replied in his letter of 1177, perhaps also wincing under the prospect of the man-eaters overrunning Italy, as suggested by John and Priest. The papal epistle is an assertion of the claims of the see of Rome to universal dominion, and it assures the Eastern Prince-Pope that his Christian professions are worthless unless he submits to the successor of Peter. 'Not every one that saith unto me Lord, Lord, shall enter into the kingdom of heaven,' quotes the Pope, and he then explains that the will of God is that every monarch and prelate should eat humble pie to the Sovereign Pontiff.

It is probable that the foundation of the whole Prester-John myth lay in the report which reached Europe of the wonderful successes of the heretical sect of Nestorianism in the East, and there seems reason to believe that the famous letter was a Nestorian fabrication with the object of exalting the East in religion and arts to an undue eminence at the expense of the West. There was indeed a foundation for the wild legends concerning a Christian empire in the East, so prevalent in Europe. Nestorius, a priest of Antioch and a disciple of St Chrysostom, was elevated by the emperor to the patriarchate of Constantinople, and in the year 428 began to propagate his heresy denying the hypostatic union. [*He maintained that the Virgin Mary should not be looked upon as the Mother of God, since she was only the mother of the man Jesus. He distinguished between Jesus the man and the Divine Person of the Word.*] The Council of Ephesus denounced him, and in spite of the emperor and court Nestorius was driven into exile. His sect spread through the East and became a flourishing Church. It reached to

China, where the emperor was all but converted; its missionaries traversed the frozen tundras of Siberia preaching their maimed gospel to the wild hordes which haunted those dreary wastes; it faced Buddhism and wrestled with it for the religious supremacy in Tibet; it established churches in Persia and in Bokhara; it penetrated India; it formed colonies in Ceylon, in Siam, and in Sumatra; so that the Catholicos or Pope of Bagdad exercised sway more extensive than that ever obtained by the successor of St Peter. The number of Christians belonging to that communion probably exceeded that of the members of the true Catholic Church in East and West.

Rubruquis the Franciscan who in 1253 was sent on a mission into Tartary was the first to let in a little light on the fable. He wrote:

The Catai dwelt beyond certain mountains across which I wandered, and in a plain in the midst of the mountains lived once an important Nestorian shepherd called Nayman. When Coir-Khan died the Nestorian people raised this man to be king and called him King Johannes, and related of him ten times as much as the truth. The Nestorians thereabouts have this way with them, that they make a great fuss about nothing, and thus they have got it noised abroad that Sartach, Mangu-Khan and Ken-Khan were Christians, simply because they treated Christians well and showed them more honour than other people. Yet in fact they were not Christians at all. And in like manner the story got about that there was a great King John. However, I traversed his pastures, and no one knew anything about him, except a few Nestorians. In his pastures lives Ken-Khan, at whose court was Brother Andrew, whom I met on my way back. This Johannes had a brother, a famous shepherd, named Unc, who lived three weeks' journey beyond the mountains of Caracatais.

This Unk-Khan was a real individual; he lost his life in the year 1203. Marco Polo, the Venetian traveller (1254-1324) identifies Unk-Khan with Prester John. [*Marco Polo found Nestorian churches along all the trade routes from Bagdad to Peking, which caused him to give Prester John great importance.*] He said: 'The Tartars, dwelling between Georgia and Bargu, had no chief of their own but paid to Prester Johannes tribute. Of the greatness of this Prester Johannes, who was properly called Un-Khan, the whole world spake; the Tartars gave him one of every ten head of cattle. When Prester John noticed that they were increasing he feared them, and planned how he could injure them. He therefore determined to scatter them, and he sent barons to do this. But the Tartars guessed what Prester John purposed . . . and they went away into the wide wastes of the North, where they might be beyond his reach.' He then goes on to relate how Genghis-Khan became the head of the Tartars and how he fought against Prester John and, after a desperate fight, overcame and slew him.

The Syriac Chronicle of the Jacobite Primate, Gregory Bar-Hebraeus (1226-1286) also identifies Unk-Khan with Prester John:

In the year of the Greeks 1514, of the Arabs 599 [*i.e.*, *A.D. 1202*], when Unk-Khan, who is the Christian King John, ruled over a stock of the barbarians Hunns called Kergis, Genghis-Khan served him with great zeal. When John observed the superiority and serviceableness of the other, he envied him and plotted to seize and murder him. But two sons of Unk-Khan, having heard this, told it to Genghis, whereupon he and his comrades fled by night and secreted themselves. Next morning Unk-Khan took possession of the Tartar tents, but found them empty. Then the party of Genghis fell upon him, and they met by the spring called Balschunah, and the side of Genghis won the day; and the followers of Unk-Khan were compelled to yield. They met again several times, till Unk-Khan was utterly discomfited and was slain himself, and his wives, sons and daughters carried into captivity. Yet we must consider that John, king of the Kergis, was not cast down for nought: nay, rather, because he had turned his heart from the fear of Christ his Lord, who had exalted him, and had taken a wife of the Zinish nation, called Quarakhata. Because he forsook the religion of his ancestors and followed strange gods, therefore God took the government from him, and gave it to one better than he, and whose heart was right before God.

3.

The Divining Rod

FROM THE REMOTEST period a rod has been regarded as the symbol of power and authority. Later, in instances quoted in the Old Testament, among the Greeks and Romans, and observed among the barbarians outside the Roman Empire, the practice grew up of some sort of divination by means of rods. At first the rods were used as an oracle which had to be skilfully interpreted. By the fifteenth century the hazel divining rod in the form that is familiar today was believed to aid the discovery of hidden treasures, veins of precious metal, springs of water, thefts and murders. By the seventeenth century the rod was in use throughout Europe and was being attacked by the Church as a devilish and blasphemous superstition as energetically as it was defended by some scientists and, of course, those who actually practised divining. The most famous case of the official use of divining at that time did not resolve the controversy as to whether the powers attributed to the rod and its operator were an authentic mystery or an incredible myth.

On 5 July 1692 at about ten o'clock in the evening, a wine-seller of Lyons and his wife were assassinated in their cellar, and their money was carried off. On the morrow, the officers of justice arrived, and examined the premises. Beside the corpses lay a large bottle wrapped in straw, and a bloody hedging bill, which undoubtedly had been the instrument used to accomplish the murder. Not a trace of those who had committed the horrible deed was to be found, and the magistrates were quite at fault as to the direction in which they should turn for a clue to the murderer or murderers.

At this juncture a neighbour reminded the magistrates of an incident which had taken place four years previously. In 1688 a theft of clothes had been made at Grenoble. In the parish of Crôle lived a man named Jacques Aymar, supposed to be endowed with the faculty of using the divining rod. This man was sent for. On reaching the spot where the theft had been committed the rod moved in his hand. He followed the track it indicated, the rod rotating between his fingers so long as he followed a certain direction, until he came to the prison gates. A magistrate gave authority for the gates to be unlocked, and Aymar approached four prisoners lately incarcerated. He ordered the four to be stood in line, and then he placed his foot on that of the first. The rod remained immovable. He passed to the second, and the rod turned at once. Before the third prisoner there were no signs. The fourth man, before being tested, confessed he was the thief, along with the second man, who also acknowledged the theft, and mentioned the name of the receiver of the stolen goods. Though he denied the theft when he was visited, Aymar recovered the property from where it was hidden. On another occasion Aymar's rod turned when he was seeking a spring of water, but digging at the spot disclosed the body of a murdered woman buried in a barrel, and the rod later identified her husband as the murderer. When these experiences were recalled, the magistrates of Lyons, at their wits' end how to discover the perpetrators of the double murder in the wine-shop, urged the Procureur du Roi to test the powers of Jacques Aymar. The fellow was sent for, and he boldly asserted his capacity for detecting criminals, if he were first brought to the spot of the murder, so as to be put *en rapport* with the murderers.

He was at once conducted to the scene of the crime with the rod in his hand. This remained stationary as he traversed the cellar, till he reached the spot where the body of the wine-seller had lain; then the stick became violently agitated, and the man's pulse rose as though he were in an access of fever. The same motions and symptoms manifested themselves when he reached the place where the other victim had lain.

Having thus received his *impression*, Aymar left the cellar, and, guided by his rod, or rather by an internal instinct, he ascended into the shop, and then stepping into the street he followed the track of the murderers like a hound upon the scent. The trail led across the court of the Archbishop's palace and down to the gate of the Rhône. It was now evening, and the city gates being all closed, the quest of blood was relinquished for the night.

Next morning Aymar returned to the scent. Accompanied by three officers he left the gate and descended the right bank of the Rhône. The rod gave indications of there having been three involved in the murder, and he pursued the traces till two of them led to a gardener's cottage. Into this he entered, and there he asserted with warmth, against the solemn denials of the proprietor, that the fugitives had entered his room, had seated themselves at his table, and had drunk wine out of one of the bottles which he indicated. Aymar tested each of the household with his rod to see if they had been in contact with the murderers. The rod moved only when over the two children, aged respectively ten and nine years. These little things, on being questioned, answered with reluctance that during their father's absence on Sunday morning, against his express commands, they had left the door open and two men, whom they described, had come in suddenly upon them and had seated themselves and made free with the bottle of wine pointed out by the diviner. This first verification of the talents of Jacques Aymar convinced some of the sceptical, but the Procurator General forbad the prosecution of the experiment till the man had been further tested.

The hedging bill discovered at the scene of the murder, smeared with blood, was unquestionably the weapon with which the crime had been committed. Three bills from the same maker and of precisely the same description were obtained, and the four were taken into a garden and secretly buried in different places. Aymar was brought in. The rod began to vibrate as his feet stood upon the place where the bloody bill was hidden. The experiment was repeated with Aymar's eyes bandaged and the bills re-buried, and there was the same result. The magistrates agreed that Aymar should be authorized to follow the trail of the murderers and have a company of archers to accompany him.

Aymar recommenced the pursuit. Continuing down the right bank of the Rhône, he came to a place half a league from the bridge of Lyons. Here the footprints of three men were observed in the sand with indications that they had entered a boat. A rowing boat was obtained, and Aymar with his escort went down the river; he found some difficulty in following the trail upon water, but with care was able to detect it. It brought him under an arch of the bridge of Vienne which boats rarely passed beneath. This proved that the fugitives were without a guide. At intervals Aymar was put ashore to test the banks with his rod and ascertain whether the murderers had landed. He discovered the places where they had slept, and indicated the chairs or benches on which they had sat. In this manner, by slow degrees he arrived at the military camp of Sablon, between Vienne and Saint-Valier. There Aymar felt violent agitation, his cheeks flushed, and his pulse beat with rapidity. He penetrated the crowds of soldiers, but did not venture to use his rod, lest the men should take it ill and fall upon him. He could not do more without special authority, and had to return to Lyons. The magistrates then provided him with the requisite powers, and he went back to the camp. But on his return he declared that the murderers were not there. He took up his pursuit again, and went down the Rhône as far as Beaucaire.

On entering the town he ascertained by means of his rod that those whom he was pursuing had parted company. He traversed several streets, then crowded on account of the annual fair, and was brought to a standstill in front of the doors of the prison. He declared that one of the murderers was inside, and he would track the others afterwards. Having obtained permission to go in, he was taken to a cell containing fourteen or fifteen prisoners. Amongst these was a hunchback who only an hour previously had been incarcerated on account of a theft he had committed at the fair. Aymar applied his rod to each of the prisoners in succession. It turned upon the hunchback. Aymar left the prison and ascertained that the other two had left Beaucaire by a little path leading into the Nismes road. Instead of following this track, he returned to Lyons with the hunchback and the guard. At Lyons a triumph awaited him. The hunchback had hitherto protested his innocence and declared that he had never set foot in Lyons. But as he was brought to that town by the way along which Aymar had determined that he had left it, the fellow was recognized at the different houses where he had lodged for the night, or stopped for food. At the little town of Bagnols he was confronted with the host and hostess of a tavern where he and his comrades had slept, and they swore to his identity, and accurately described his companions: their description tallied with that given by the children of the gardener. The wretched man was so confounded by this recognition that he admitted having stayed there a few days before, along with two Provençals. These men, he said, were the criminals; he had been their servant, and had only kept guard in the upper room whilst they committed the murders in the cellar.

On his arrival at Lyons he was committed to prison, and his trial was decided upon. At his first interrogation he told his tale precisely as he had related it before, with these additions: the murderers spoke patois and had purchased two bills. At ten o'clock in the evening all three had gone into the wine-shop. The Provençals had a large bottle wrapped in straw, and they persuaded the publican and his wife to go down with them into the cellar whilst he, the hunchback, acted as watch in the shop. The two men murdered the wine-seller and his wife with their bills, and then went up to the shop, where they opened the coffer and stole from it 130 crowns, eight Louis d'ors, and a silver belt. The crime accomplished, they took refuge in the court of a large house – this was the Archbishop's palace indicated by Aymar – and passed the night in it. Next day, early, they left Lyons and only stopped for a moment at a gardener's cottage. Some way down the river they found a boat moored to the bank. They went down river in it and came ashore at the spot which Aymar had pointed out. They stayed some days in the camp at Sablon, and then went on to Beaucaire.

Aymar was now sent in quest of the other murderers. He took up their trail at the gate of Beaucaire. One track led him to the prison doors of Beaucaire. He asked to be allowed to search among the prisoners for this man. This time he was mistaken. The second fugitive was not inside, but the gaoler confirmed that a man whom he described – and his description tallied with the known appearance of one of the Provençals – had called at the gate shortly after the removal of the hunchback to enquire after him, and on learning of his removal to Lyons had hurried off precipitately. Aymar now followed his track from the prison, and this brought him to that of the third criminal. He pursued the double scent for some days. But it became evident that the two culprits had become alarmed at what had transpired in Beaucaire, and were fleeing from France. Aymar traced them to the frontier, and then returned to Lyons.

On 30 August 1692 the poor hunchback was, according to sentence, broken on the wheel in the Place des Terreaux. On his way to execution he had to pass the wine-shop. There the recorder publicly read his sentence, which had been delivered by thirty judges. The criminal knelt and asked pardon of the poor wretches in whose murder he was involved, after which he continued his course to the place fixed for his execution.

There are five contemporary authoritative accounts of this extraordinary story. M. Chauvin, Doctor of Medicine, published a *Lettre à Mme. la Marquise de Senozan, sur les moyens dont on s'est servi pour découvrir les complices d'un assassinat commis à Lyon, le 5 juillet, 1692*, Lyons, 1692. The *procès-verbal* of the Procureur du Roi, M. de Vanini, is also extant, and published in the *Physique occulte* of the Abbé de Vallemont. Pierre Garnier, Doctor of Medicine of the University of Montpelier, wrote a *Dissertation physique en forme de lettre, à M. de Sève, seigneur de Fléchères*, on Jacques Aymar, printed the same year at Lyons and republished in the *Histoire critique des pratiques superstitieuses, du Père Lebrun*. The Abbé Lagarde wrote a careful account of the whole transaction. In a letter printed by Lebrun in his *Histoire critique* cited above, the Abbé Bignon told of experiments conducted at the murder site with responsible witnesses including another man who had the power to use the rod. The Sieur Pauthot, Dean of the College of Medicine at Lyons printed an eye-witness account of the behaviour of Aymar in the cellar 'which he shrank from entering, because he felt violent agitations which overcame him when he used the rod over the place where the corpses had lain.' When Aymar passed the rod over these spots

the stick rotated with such violence that it seemed easier to break than to stop it. The peasant then quitted our company to faint away, as was his wont after similar experiments. I followed him. He turned very pale and broke into a profuse perspiration, whilst for a quarter of an hour his pulse was violently troubled; indeed the faintness was so considerable that they were obliged to dash water in his face and give him water to drink in order to bring him round.

4.

The Seven Sleepers of Ephesus

ONE OF THE MOST picturesque myths of ancient days, which has its parallel in the mythologies of many civilisations, is told in its Christian version by Jacques de Voragine in his *Legenda Aurea*:

The seven sleepers were natives of Ephesus [*the ancient city in Asia Minor where St Paul once stayed for two years and later re-visited: its ruins are 35 miles from the Turkish port of Izmir, or Smyrna*]. The Emperor Decius [*reigned from Rome A.D. 249-251*], who persecuted the Christians, having come to Ephesus, ordered the erection of temples in the city, that all might come and sacrifice before him, and he commanded that the Christians should be sought out and given their choice, either to worship the idols or to die. So great was the consternation in the city that friends denounced friends, fathers their sons and sons their fathers.

Now there were in Ephesus seven Christians: Maximian, Malchus, Marcian, Dionysius, John, Serapion and Constantine by name. They refused to sacrifice to the idols, and remained in their houses praying and fasting. They were accused before Decius, and they confessed themselves to be Christians. However, the emperor gave them a little time to consider what line they would adopt. They took advantage of this reprieve to dispense their goods among the poor, and then they retired, all seven, to Mount Celion, where they determined to conceal themselves.

One of their number, Malchus, in the disguise of a physician, went to the town to obtain victuals. Decius, who had been absent from Ephesus for a little while, returned and gave orders for the seven to be sought. Malchus, having escaped from the town, fled, full of fear, to his comrades and told them of the emperor's fury. They were much alarmed, and Malchus handed them the loaves he had bought, bidding them eat so that, fortified by the food, they might have courage in the time of trial. They ate, and then, as they sat weeping and speaking to one another, by the will of God they fell asleep.

The Pagans sought everywhere but could not find them, and Decius was greatly irritated at their escape. He had their parents brought before him, and threatened them with death if they did not reveal the place of concealment. But they could only answer that the seven young men had distributed their goods to the poor, and that they were quite ignorant as to their whereabouts.

Decius, thinking it possible that they might be hiding in a cavern, blocked up the mouth with stones intending them to perish from hunger.

Three hundred and sixty years passed*, and in the thirtieth year of the reign of Theodosius [*Theodosius II, ruled the Byzantine empire from Constantinople 408-450*] there broke forth a heresy denying the resurrection of the dead . . .

Now it happened that an Ephesian was building a stable on the side of Mount Celion, and finding a pile of stones handy, he took them for his edifice, and thus opened the mouth of the cave. Then the seven sleepers awoke, and it was to them as if they had slept but a single night. They began to ask Malchus what decision Decius had given concerning them.

'He is going to hunt us down, so as to force us to sacrifice to the idols,' was the reply. 'God knows,' said Maximian, 'we shall never do that.' Then, giving new heart to his companions, he urged Malchus to go back to the town to buy some more bread and at the same time obtain fresh information. Malchus took five coins and left the cavern. On seeing the stones he was filled with astonishment. However, he went on towards the city. But what was his bewilderment, on approaching the gate, to see over it a cross! He went to another gate and there he saw the same sacred sign, and he observed it thus over each gate of the city. He believed he must be experiencing the after-effects of a dream.

Then he entered Ephesus, rubbing his eyes, and he walked to a baker's shop. He heard people using our Lord's name, and he was the more perplexed. 'Yesterday no one dared pronounce the name of Jesus, and now it is on every one's lips. Wonderful! I can hardly believe myself to be in Ephesus.' He asked a passer-by the name of the city, and on being told it was Ephesus he was thunderstruck. He came to the baker's shop and laid down his money. The baker, examining the coin, inquired whether he had

* The mediaeval chronicler's arithmetic was faulty. It was about half this time.

found a treasure, and began to whisper to some others in the shop. The youth, thinking that he was discovered and they were about to conduct him to the emperor, implored them to let him alone, offering to leave loaves and money if only he could be allowed to escape. But the shop-men, seizing him, said: 'Whoever you are, you have found a treasure. Show us where it is so that we can share it with you, and then we will hide you.' Malchus was too frightened to answer. So they put a rope round his neck and led him through the streets into the market-place. The news soon spread that the young man had discovered a great treasure, and soon there was a vast crowd around him. He stoutly protested his innocence. No one recognized him, and his eyes ranging over the faces which surrounded him could not see one which he had known, or which was in the slightest degree familiar to him.

St Martin, the bishop, and Antipater, the governor, having heard of the excitement, ordered the young man to be brought before them along with the bakers.

The bishop and the governor asked him where he had found the treasure, and he replied that he had found none, but that the few coins were from his own purse. He was next asked whence he came. He replied that he was a native of Ephesus, 'if this be Ephesus.'

'Send for your relations – your parents, if they live here,' ordered the governor.

'They live here certainly,' replied the youth, and he mentioned their names. No such names were known in the town. Then the governor exclaimed: 'How dare you say that this money belonged to your parents when it dates back three hundred and seventy-seven years [*according to modern historical knowledge, 188 years*] and is as old as the beginning of the reign of Decius, and is utterly unlike our modern coinage? Do you think you can impose on the old men and the sages of Ephesus? Believe me, I shall make you suffer the severities of the law unless you show me where you made the discovery.'

'I implore you,' cried Malchus, 'in the name of God, answer me a few questions and then I will answer yours. Where is the Emperor Decius gone to?'

The bishop answered: 'My son, there is no emperor of that name. He who was thus called died long ago.'

Malchus replied: 'Everything I hear perplexes me more and more. Follow me, and I will show you my comrades, who fled with me into a cave of Mount Celion only yesterday to escape the cruelty of Decius. I will lead you to them.'

This bishop turned to the governor. 'The hand of God is here,' he said. Then they followed, and a great crowd after them. And Malchus entered first into the cavern to join his companions, and the bishop followed . . .

And there they saw the martyrs seated in the cave, with their faces fresh and blooming as roses.

So all fell down and glorified God. The bishop and the governor sent notice to Theodosius, and he hurried to Ephesus. All the inhabitants met him and conducted him to the cavern. As soon as the saints beheld the emperor their faces shone like the sun, and the emperor gave thanks unto God and embraced them, and said: 'I see you as though I saw the Saviour restoring Lazarus.' Maximian replied: 'Believe us! For the faith's sake, God has resuscitated us before the great resurrection day in order that you may firmly believe in the resurrection of the dead. For as the child is in its mother's womb living and not suffering, so have we lived without suffering, fast asleep.'

And having this spoken, they bowed their heads, and their souls returned to their Maker.

The emperor, rising, bent over them and embraced them, weeping. He gave orders for golden reliquaries to be made. But that night they appeared to him in a dream, and said that hitherto they had slept in the earth, and that in the earth they desired to sleep on till God should raise them again.

Such is the beautiful story. It seems to have travelled to us from the East. Jacobus Sarugiensis, a Mesopotamian bishop in the fifth or sixth century, is said to have been the first to commit it to writing. Gregory of Tours (*De Glor. Mart. i. 9*) was perhaps the first to introduce it to Europe. Dionysius of Antioch told the story in Syrian in the ninth century, and Photius of Constantinople reproduced it with the remark that Mahomet had adapted it into the Koran. (Mahomet made the Sleepers prophesy his coming and he gave them a dog named Kratim which sleeps with them and which is endowed with the gift of prophecy. This dog is one of the ten animals to be admitted into his paradise, along with Jonah's whale, Solomon's ant, Ishmael's ram, Abraham's calf, the Queen of Sheba's ass, the prophet Salech's camel, Moses's ox, Belkis's cuckoo, and Mahomet's ass.) Metaphrastus alludes to the tale of the Seven Sleepers, and in the tenth century Eutychius inserted it into his annals of Arabia. It is found in the Coptic and Maronite books, and among early historians Paulus Diaconus, Nicephorus and others have included it in their works.

In England, William of Malmesbury recorded that Edward the Confessor, musing on divine things at an Easter banquet, suddenly burst out laughing and afterwards explained to Earl Harold that he had seen the Seven Sleepers of Ephesus, who had been slumbering two hundred years in a cave of Mount Celion lying always on their right sides, suddenly turn themselves over on their left sides, and he could not prevent himself from laughing. Earl Harold sent a knight with a clerk and a monk to the emperor at Constantinople with letters and presents from King Edward and a request to be admitted into the cave of the sleepers. The Ephesians declared that they knew from their forefathers that the Seven had always lain on their right sides. But when the Englishmen went into the cave they were all found lying on their left sides. This was taken as a warning of the miseries which were to befall Christendom through the inroads of the Saracens, Turks and Tartars. For whenever sorrow threatens, the Sleepers turn on their sides.

It was perhaps too much to ask that the Seven Sleepers should be left to rest in earth. At the height of the veneration of saintly relics their remains were conveyed to Marseilles in a large stone sarcophagus which is still exhibited in St Victor's church.

The story of long sleepers, often seven in number dates from heathen mythology and was baptized by Christian hands. The Greeks believed that Endymion had been preserved in unfading youth and beauty by the gift of perpetual sleep. Pliny relates a similar story of Epimenides, one of the seven ancient sages who flourished in the time of Solon. The Scandinavian Siegfrid, the Frankish Charlemagne, the Danish Ogier, all sleep waiting to wake and avenge the blood of the saints. Frederic Barbarossa sleeps with his six knights within the great Kyffhäuserberg in Thuringia. Even in Scotland Thomas of Erceldoune sleeps beneath the Eildon hills. In Ireland Brian Boroimhe slumbers awaiting the call to come to his country's aid, and in Wales Arthur still sleeps through the long dream of Avalon. I believe that the mythological core of this picturesque legend is the repose of the earth through the seven winter months.

5.

𝕎illiam 𝕋ell

I SUPPOSE THAT MOST people regard the story of Tell and the apple as an historical event, and when they undertake the regular Swiss round they visit the market-place of Altorf, where the site of the lime-tree to which Tell's child was bound is pointed out to them, with the statue which is asserted to mark the spot where Tell stood to take aim. Once, indeed, there stood another monument erected near Lucerne in commemoration of this event: a wooden obelisk painted to look like granite, surmounted by a rosy-cheeked apple transfixed by a golden arrow. This gingerbread memorial of bad taste has perished, struck by lightning. I shall in the following pages demolish the very story which that erection was intended to commemorate.

It is almost too well known to need repetition.

In the year 1307, Gessler, Vogt [*local governor*] of the Emperor Albert of Hapsburg, set a hat on a pole as symbol of imperial power, and ordered every one who passed by to do obeisance towards it. A mountaineer of the name of Tell boldly crossed the space before it without saluting the hated symbol. By Gessler's command he was at once seized and brought before him. As Tell was known to be an expert archer, he was ordered by way of punishment to shoot an apple off the head of his own son. Finding remonstrance vain, he submitted. The apple was placed on the child's head, Tell bent his bow, the arrow sped, and apple and arrow fell to the ground together. But the

Vogt noticed that Tell, before shooting, had stuck another arrow into his belt, and he enquired the reason.

'It was for you,' replied the sturdy archer. 'Had I shot my child, know that it would not have missed your heart.'

This event, it should be observed, took place in the beginning of the fourteenth century. But Saxo Grammaticus, a Danish writer of the twelfth century, tells the story of a hero of his own country, who lived in the tenth century. He relates the incident as follows:

Toki, who had for some time been in the king's service, had by his deeds, surpassing those of his comrades, made enemies by his virtues. One day, when he had drunk too much, he boasted to those who sat at table with him that his skill in archery was such that with the first shot of an arrow he could hit the smallest apple set on top of a stick at a considerable distance. His detractors, hearing this, lost no time in conveying what he had said to the king (Harald Bluetooth). But the wickedness of this monarch soon transformed the confidence of the father to the jeopardy of the son, for he ordered the dearest pledge of his life to stand in place of the stick, and decreed that if the utterer of the boast did not at his first shot strike down the apple he should pay with his head the penalty of having made an idle boast. As soon as the boy was led forth Toki carefully admonished him to receive the whir of the arrow as calmly as possible, with attentive ears and without moving his head, lest by a slight motion of the body he should frustrate the experience of his well-tried skill. He also made him stand with his back towards him, lest he should be frightened at the sight of the arrow. Then he drew three arrows from his quiver, and the very first he shot struck the proposed mark. Toki being asked by the king why he had taken so many more arrows out of his quiver, when he was to make but one trial with his bow, replied: 'That I might avenge on thee the error of the first, by the points of the others, lest my innocence might happen to be afflicted, and thy injustice go unpunished,

The same incident is told of Egil, brother of the mythical Velundr, in the Saga of Thidrik.

In Norwegian history it also appears with variations again and again. It is told of King Olaf the Saint, who died in 1030, that, desiring the conversion of a brave heathen named Eindridi, he competed with him in various athletic sports. He swam with him, wrestled, and then shot with him. The king dared Eindridi to strike a writing-tablet from off his son's head with an arrow. Eindridi prepared to attempt the difficult shot. The king bade two men bind the eyes of the child and hold the napkin, so that he should not move when he heard the whistle of the arrow. The king aimed first, and the arrow grazed the lad's head. Eindridi then prepared to shoot, but the mother of the boy interfered, and persuaded the king to abandon this dangerous test of skill. In this version also, Eindridi is prepared to revenge himself on the king, should the child be injured.

But a closer approximation still to the Tell myth is found in the life of Hemingr, another Norse archer who was challenged by King Harald, who died in 1066. The story runs as herewith recounted.

The island was densely overgrown with wood, and the people went into the forest. The king took a spear and set it with its point in the soil, then he laid an arrow on the string and shot up into the air. The arrow turned in the air and came down upon the spear-shaft and stood up in it. Hemingr took another arrow and shot up. His was lost to sight for some time, but it came back and pierced the nick of the king's arrow . . . Then the king took a knife and stuck it into an oak. He next drew his bow and planted an arrow in the haft of the knife. Thereupon Hemingr took his arrows. The king stood by him and said: 'They are all inlaid with gold, you are a capital workman.' Hemingr answered: 'They are not of my manufacture, but are presents.' He shot, and his arrow cleft the haft, and the point entered the socket of the blade.

'We must have a keener contest,' said the king, taking an arrow and flushing with anger. Then he laid the arrow on the string and drew his bow to the farthest, so that the horns were nearly brought to meet. Away flashed the arrow, and pierced a tender twig. All said that this was a most astonishing feat of dexterity. But Hemingr shot from a greater distance and split a hazel nut. All were astonished to see this. Then said the king: 'Take a nut and set it on the head of your brother Bjorn, and aim at it from precisely the same distance. If you miss the mark, then your life goes.'

Hemingr answered: 'Sire, my life is at your disposal, but I will not adventure that shot.' Then out spoke Bjorn: 'Shoot, brother, rather than die yourself.' Hemingr said 'Have you the pluck to stand quite still without shrinking?' 'I will do my best.' said Bjorn. 'Then let the king stand by,' said Hemingr, 'and let him see whether I touch the nut'.

The king agreed, and bade Oddr Ufeig's son stand by Bjorn and see that the shot was fair. Hemingr then went to the spot fixed for him by the king, and signed himself with the cross, saying: 'God be my witness that I had rather die myself than injure my brother Bjorn; let all the blame rest on King Harald.'

Then Hemingr flung his spear. The spear went straight to the mark and passed between the nut and the crown of the lad, who was not in the least injured. It flew further, and stopped not till it fell . . .

Years afterwards, this risk was avenged upon the hard-hearted monarch. In the battle of Stamford Bridge an arrow from a skilled archer penetrated the wind-pipe of the king, and it is supposed to have sped, observes the Saga writer, from the bow of Hemingr, then in the service of the English monarch.

The 'William Tell' story is found in different versions scattered through countries as remote as Persia and Iceland, Switzerland and Finland. This proves, I think, that it can in no way be regarded as history, but is rather one of the numerous household myths common to the whole stock of Aryan nations. Mythologists will, I suppose, consider the myth to represent the manifestation of some natural phenomena, and the individuals of the story to be impersonifications of natural forces. The Tell myth has no such immediate significance, and though it is possible that Gessler and Harald may be the power of evil and darkness, and the bold archer the storm-cloud with his arrow of lightning and his iris bow, bent against the sun, which is resting like a coin or a golden apple on the edge of the horizon, yet we have no guarantee that such an interpretation is not an over-straining of a theory.

6.

𝕿𝖍𝖊 𝕯𝖔𝖌 𝕲𝖊𝖑𝖑𝖊𝖗𝖙

HAVING DEMOLISHED the story of the famous shot of William Tell, I proceed to the destruction of another article of popular belief.

Who that has visited Snowdon has not seen the grave of Llewellyn's faithful hound Gellert, and been told by the guide the touching story of the death of the noble animal? How can we doubt the facts, seeing that the place, Beth-Gellert, is named after the dog, and that the grave is still visible? But unfortunately for the truth of the legend, its pedigree can be traced with the utmost precision.

The story is as follows:

The Welsh Prince Llewellyn had a noble deerhound, Gellert, whom he trusted to watch the cradle of his baby son whilst he himself was absent.

One day, on his return, to his intense horror, he beheld the cradle empty and upset, the clothes dabbled with blood, and Gellert's mouth dripping with gore. Concluding hastily that the hound had proved unfaithful, had fallen on the child and devoured it, in a paroxysm of rage the prince drew his sword and slew the dog. Next instant the cry of the babe from behind the cradle showed him that the child was uninjured, and on looking further Llewellyn discovered the body of a huge wolf, which had entered the house to seize and devour the child, but which had been kept off and killed by the brave Gellert.

In his self-reproach and grief, the prince erected a stately monument to Gellert, and called the place where he was buried after the poor hound's name.

Now I find in Russia precisely the same story told with just the same appearance of truth about a Czar Piras. In Germany it appears with considerable variations. A man determines on slaying his old dog Sultan, and consults with his wife how this is to be effected. Sultan overhears the conversation, and complains bitterly to the wolf, who suggests an ingenious plan by which the master may be induced to spare the dog. Next day, when the man is going to his work, the wolf undertakes to carry off the child from its cradle. Sultan is to attack him and rescue the infant. The plan succeeds admirably, and the dog spends his remaining years in comfort. (*Grimm, K.M.* 48.)

But there is a story in closer conformity to that of Gellert among the French collections of *fabliaux* made by Le Grand d' Aussey and Edélèstand du Méril. It became popular through the *Gesta Romanorum*, a collection of tales made by the monks for harmless reading in the fourteenth century.

In the *Gesta* the tale is told as follows:

Folliculus, a knight, was fond of hunting and tournaments. He had only one son, for whom three nurses were provided. Next to this child, he loved his falcon and his greyhound. It happened one day that he was called to a tournament, to which his wife and domestics also went, leaving the child in the cradle, the greyhound lying by him and the falcon on his perch. A serpent that inhabited a hole near the castle, taking advantage of the profound silence that reigned, crept from his habitation and advanced towards the cradle to devour the child. The falcon, perceiving the danger, fluttered with his wings till he awoke the dog, who instantly attacked the invader, and after a fierce conflict in which he was sorely wounded, killed him. He then lay down on the ground to lick and heal his wounds. When the nurses returned they found the cradle overturned, the child thrown out, and the ground covered in blood, as was also the dog, who they immediately concluded had killed the child.

Terrified at the idea of meeting the anger of the parents, they determined to escape. But in their flight they fell in with their mistress, to whom they were compelled to relate the supposed murder of the child by the greyhound. The knight soon arrived to hear the sad story and, maddened with fury, rushed toward the spot. The poor wounded and faithful animal made an effort to rise and welcome his master with his accustomed fondness, but the enraged knight received him on the point of his sword, and he fell lifeless to the ground. On examination of the cradle the infant was found alive and unhurt, with the dead serpent lying by him. The knight now perceived what had happened, lamented bitterly over his faithful dog, and blamed himself for having too hastily depended on the words of his wife. Abandoning the profession of arms, he broke his lance in pieces, and vowed a pilgrimage to the Holy Land, where he spent the rest of his days in peace.

The monkish hit at the wife is amusing, and might have been supposed to have originated with those determined misogynists, as the gallant Welshmen lay all the blame on the man. But the good compilers of the *Gesta* wrote little of their own, except moral applications of the tales they relate, and the story of Folliculus and his dog, like many others in their collection, is drawn from a foreign source.

It occurs in the Seven Wise Masters and in the *Calumnia Novercalis* as well, so that it must have been popular throughout mediaeval Europe. Now the tales of the Seven Wise Masters are translations from a Hebrew work, the Kalilah and Dimnah of Rabbi Joel, composed about A.D. 1250, or from Symeon Seth's Greek Kylile and Dimne, written in 1080. These Greek and Hebrew works were derived from kindred sources. That of Rabbi Joel was a translation from an Arabic version made in the twelfth century by Nasr-Allah, whilst Symeon Seth's was a translation of the Persian Kalilah and Dimnah. But this Persian version, in turn, was not an original work, but a translation from the Sanskrit Pantschatantra, made about A.D. 540.

In this ancient Indian book the story runs as follows:

A Brahmin named Devasaman had a wife, who gave birth to a son and also to an ichneumon [*an animal like a weasel, allied to the mongoose*]. She loved both her children dearly, giving them alike the breast, and anointing them alike with salves. But she feared the ichneumon might not love his brother.

One day, having laid her boy in bed, she took up the water jar and said to her husband: 'Hear, my master! I am going to the tank to fetch water. Whilst I am absent watch the boy, lest he gets injured by the ichneumon.' After she had left the house the Brahmin went forth begging, leaving the house open. In crept a black snake, and attempted to bite the child. But the ichneumon rushed at it and tore it to pieces. Then, proud of its achievement, it sallied forth, all bloody, to meet its mother. She, seeing the creature stained with blood, concluded with feminine precipitance that it had fallen on the baby and killed it, and she flung her water jar at it and slew it. Only on her return home did she ascertain her mistake.

The same story is also told in the Hitopadesa (iv. 13) but the animal is an otter, not an ichneumon. In the Arabic version a weasel takes the place of the ichneumon.

The Buddhist missionaries carried the story into Mongolia, and in the Mongolian Uligerun, which is a translation of the Tibetan Dsanglun, the story re-appears with the pole-cat as the brave and suffering defender of the child.

Stanislaus Julien, the great Chinese scholar, has discovered the same tale in the Chinese work entitled *The Forest of Pearls from the Garden of the Law*. This work dates from 668, and in it the creature is an ichneumon.

In the Persian *Sindibad-nâmeeh* there is the same tale, but the faithful animal is a cat. In Sandabar and Syntipas it has become a dog. Through the influence of Sandabar on the Hebrew translation of the Kalilah and Dimnah, the ichneumon is also replaced by a dog.

Such is the history of the Gellert legend. It is an introduction into Europe from India, every step of its transmission being clearly demonstrable. From the *Gesta Romanorum* it passed into a popular tale throughout Europe, and in different countries it was, like the Tell legend, localized and individualized. Many a Welsh story, such as those contained in the Mabinogion, are as easily traced to an Eastern origin.

But every story has its root. The root of the Gellert tale is this: A man forms an alliance of friendship with a beast or bird. The dumb animal renders him a signal service. He misunderstands the act, and kills his preserver.

We have tracked this myth under the Gellert form from India to Wales. But under another form it is the property of the whole Aryan family, and forms a portion of the traditional lore of all nations sprung from that stock.

Thence across to the classic fable of the peasant who, as he slept, was bitten by a fly. He awoke, and in a rage killed the insect. Too late, he observed that the little creature had aroused him so that he might avoid a snake which lay coiled up near his pillow.

In the Anvar-i-Suhaili there is a kindred tale: A king had a falcon. One day, whilst hunting, he filled a goblet with water dripping from a rock. As he put the vessel to his lips, his falcon dashed upon it and upset it with its wings. The king, in a fury, slew the bird, and then discovered that the water dripped from the jaws of a serpent of the most poisonous nature.

This story, with some variations, occurs in Aesop, Aelian and Apthonius. In the Greek fable a peasant liberates an eagle from the clutches of a dragon. The dragon squirts poison into the water which the peasant is about to drink. The grateful eagle upsets the goblet with its wings.

The story appears in Egypt under a whimsical form. A Wali [*provincial governor*] once smashed a pot full of herbs which a cook had prepared. The exasperated cook thrashed the well-intentioned but unfortunate Wali within an inch of his life, and when he returned, exhausted with his efforts at belabouring the man, he examined the broken pot and discovered amongst the herbs a poisonous snake.

How many brothers, sisters, uncles, aunts and cousins of all degrees a little story has! There is scarcely a story which I hear which I cannot connect with some family of myths, and whose pedigree I cannot ascertain with more or less precision. Shakespeare drew the plots of his plays from Boccaccio or Straparola; but these Italians did not invent the tales they lent to the English dramatist. King Lear does not originate with Geoffrey of Monmouth, but comes from early Indian stores of fable, whence also are derived the Merchant of Venice and the pound of flesh and the very incident of the three caskets. Who would credit it, were it not proved by conclusive facts, that British legends are the inheritance of the whole family of Aryan nations, and that Peeping Tom of Coventry peeped in India and on the Tartar steppes before Lady Godiva was born?

7.

Tailed Men

I WELL REMEMBER having it impressed upon me by a Devon-shire nurse, as a little child, that all Cornishmen were born with tails. This feature was asserted of certain men of Kent in olden times, and was attributed to Divine vengeance on them for having insulted St Thomas à Becket, if we may believe Polydore Vergil. 'There were some,' he says,

to whom it seemed that the king's secret wish was that Thomas should be got rid of. He indeed, as one accounted to be an enemy of the king's person, was already regarded with so little respect, nay, was treated with so much contempt, that when he came to Strood, which village is situated on the Medway, the river that washes Rochester, the inhabitants of the place, being eager to show some mark of contumely to the prelate in his disgrace, did not scruple to cut off the tail of the horse on which he was riding. But by this profane and inhospitable act they covered themselves with eternal reproach, for it so happened after this, by the will of God, that all the off-spring born from the men who had done this thing were born with tails like brute animals. But this mark of infamy, which formerly was every-where notorious, has disappeared with the extinction of the race whose fathers perpetrated this deed.

John Bale, the zealous reformer, Bishop of Ossory in Edward VI's time, refers to this story, and also mentions a variation of the scene and cause of this ignoble punishment. He writes, quoting his authorities:

John Capgrave and Alexander of Esseby saith that of casting of fish tails at this Augustine, Dorsetshire men had tails ever after. But Polydorus applieth it unto Kentish men at Stroud, by Rochester, for cutting off Thomas Becket's horse's tail. Thus hath England in all other lands a perpetual infamy of tails by they written legends of lies, yet can they not well tell where to bestow them truly. In the legends of their sanctified sorcerers they have defamed the English posterity with tails. That an Englishman now cannot travel in another land by way of merchandise or any other honest occupying, but it is most contumeliously thrown in his teeth that all Englishmen have tails. That uncomely note and report have the nation gotten, without recover, by these lazy and idle lubbers, the monks and priests, which could find no matters to advance their canonized gains by, or their saints, as they call them, but manifest lies and knaveries.' (*Actes of English Votaries.*)

Lord Monboddo, a Scotch judge of the last [*eighteenth*] century and a philosopher of some repute, though of great eccentricity, stoutly maintained the theory that man ought to have a tail, and that the abrupt termination of the spine without caudal elongation is a sad blemish in the organisation of man. The tail, the point in which man is inferior to the brute, what a delicate index of the mind it is! How it expresses the passions of love and hate, how nicely it gives token of the feelings of joy or fear which animate the soul! Dr Johnson paid a visit to the judge, and knocked on the head his theory that men ought to have tails and actually were born with them occasionally. For, said he, 'Of a standing fact, sir, there ought to be no controversy. If there are men with tails, catch a *homo caudatus* [*tailed man*].' And again, 'It is a pity to see Lord Monboddo publish such notions as he has done; a man of sense and of so much elegant learning. There would be a little in a fool doing it; we should only laugh; but when a wise man does it we are sorry. Other people have strange notions, but they conceal them. If they have tails, they hide them. But Monboddo is as jealous of his tail as a squirrel.'

John Struys, a Dutch traveller who visited the isle of Formosa in 1677, wrote of a murder which took place there and the subsequent arrest of the murderer:

As the crime was so atrocious, and, if allowed to pass with impunity, might entail even more serious consequences, it was determined to burn the man. He was tied up to a stake, where he was kept for some hours before the time of execution arrived. It was then that I beheld what I had never thought to see. He had a tail more than a foot long, covered with red

hair, and very like that of a cow. When he saw the surprise that this discovery created among the European spectators, he informed us that his
tail was the effect of climate, for all the inhabitants of the southern side of
the island, where they then were, were provided with like appendages.

Hornemann reported that between the Gulf of Benin and
Abyssinia there were tailed cannibals, named by the natives *Niam-
niams*; and in 1849 M. Descouret, on his return from Mecca, affirmed
that such was the common report. Mr Harrison in his *Highlands of
Ethiopia* alludes to the common belief among the Abyssinians in a
pigmy race of this nature. MM. Arnault and Vayssière, travellers in
the same country in 1850, brought the subject before the Academy of
Sciences. In 1851 M. de Castelnau gave additional details of an
expedition against these tailed men. 'The Niam-niams,' he said,
'were sleeping in the sun. The Haoussas approached, and, falling on
them, massacred them to the last man. They had all of them tails
forty centimetres long and from two to three in diameter. This organ
is smooth. Among the corpses were those of several women, who
were deformed in the same manner. M. d'Abbadie, another Abyssinian traveller, gave a contradictory account on some details from
the lips of an Abyssinian priest: 'At the distance of fifteen days'
journey south of Herrar is a place where all the men have tails, the
length of a palm, covered with hair at the extremity of the spine. The
females of that country are very beautiful and tailless. I have seen
some fifteen of these people at Besberah, and I am positive that the
tail is natural.'

Dr Wolf declared in his *Travels and Adventures*, Vol. II, 1861, 'I
heard from a great many Abyssinians and Armenians, and I am
convinced of the truth of it, that there are near Narea in Abyssinia
men and women with large tails with which they are able to knock
down a horse, and there are also such people near China. In the
College of Surgeons at Dublin may be still seen a human skeleton
with a tail seven inches long! There are many known instances of this
elongation of the caudal vertebra, as in the Poonangs in Borneo.'
The most circumstantial account of the Niam-niams is given by
Dr Hubsch, physician to the hospitals of Constantinople. 'It was in
1852,' says he,

that I saw for the first time a tailed negress. I was struck by this pheno-
menon, and I questioned her master, a slave-dealer. I learned from him
that there exists a tribe called Niam-niam, occupying the interior of Africa.

All the members of this tribe bear the caudal appendage, and, as Oriental imagination is given to exaggeration, I was assured that the tails sometimes attained the length of two feet. That which I observed was smooth and hairless. It was about two inches long, and terminated in a point . . . The woman's master had been unable to sell her over a period of six months, notwithstanding the low figure he asked. The abhorrence with which she was regarded was not attributed to her tail, but to the partiality, which she was unable to conceal, for human flesh. Her tribe fed on the flesh of the prisoners taken from neighbouring tribes, with whom they were constantly at war. As soon as one of the tribe dies his relations, instead of burying him, cut him up and regale themselves upon his remains; consequently there are no cemeteries in this land . . .

According to a North-American Indian tradition all men were created originally with long-haired, sleek and comely tails. These tails were their delight, and they adorned them with paint, beads and wampum. Then the world was at peace; discord and wars were unknown. Men became proud and forgot their maker, and He found it necessary to disturb their serenity by sending them a scourge which might teach them humility, and make them realize their dependence on the Great Spirit. Then He amputated their tails, and out of these discarded members fashioned women – who, say the Kikapoos, retain traces of their origin, for we find them always trailing after men, frisky and impulsive. (Atherne Jones, *Trad. N. American Indians*, iii, 175.)

Yet, notwithstanding all this testimony in favour of tailed men and women, I profess myself dubious, and shall yield only when a *homo caudatus* has been caught and shown to me.

8.

Antichrist and Pope Joan

From the earliest days of the Church the advent of the Man of Sin has been looked forward to with terror, and the passages of Scripture relating to him have been studied with solemn awe, lest that day of wrath should come upon the Church unawares. As events in the world's history took place which seemed to be indications of the approach of Antichrist, a great horror fell upon men's minds and their imaginations conjured up myths which flew from mouth to mouth and which were implicitly believed.

In the time of Antichrist, we are told by ancient Commentators, the Church will be divided. One portion will hold to the world-power, the other will seek out the old paths and cling to the only true Guide. The high places will be filled with unbelievers in the Incarnation, and the Church will be in a condition of the utmost spiritual degradation, but enjoying the highest State patronage. The religion in favour will be one of morality, but not of dogma; and the Man of Sin will be able to promulgate his doctrine, according to St Anselm, through his great eloquence and wisdom, his vast learning and mightiness in the Holy Scriptures, which he will wrest to the overthrowing of dogma. He will be liberal in bribes, for he will be of unbounded wealth. He will be capable of performing 'great signs and wonders' so as 'to deceive the very elect'. And at the last he will tear the moral veil from his countenance and, a monster of impiety and cruelty, he will inaugurate that awful persecution, which is to last for three years and a half and to excel in horror all the persecutions which have gone before. In that terrible season of confusion faith will be all but extinguished. But still the Church will remain unwrecked. She will weather the storm. She will come forth 'beautiful as the moon, terrible as an army with banners.' For after the lapse of those three and a half years Christ will descend to avenge the blood of the saints by destroying Antichrist and the world-power.

Such was the Scriptural doctrine of Antichrist as held by the Early and Mediaeval Church. It gave rise to many myths among the vulgar and the imaginative. Rabanus Maurus, in his work on the life of Antichrist, gives a full account of the miracles he will perform. He tells us that the Man-fiend will heal the sick, raise the dead, restore sight to the blind, hearing to the deaf, speech to the dumb. He will raise storms and calm them, will remove mountains, make trees flourish or wither at a word. He will rebuild the temple at Jerusalem and make the Holy City the great capital of the world. Popular opinion added that his vast wealth would be obtained from hidden treasures which are now being concealed by the demons for his use. Various possessed persons, when interrogated, announced that such was the case, and that the amount of buried gold was vast.

'In the year 1599,' says Canon Moreau, a contemporary historian, 'a rumour circulated with prodigious rapidity through Europe that Antichrist had been born at Babylon, and that already the Jews of that part were hurrying to receive and recognize him as their Messiah. The news came from Italy and Germany, and was extended to Spain, England and other Western kingdoms, troubling many people, even the most discreet. However, the learned gave it no credence, saying that the signs predicted in Scripture to precede that event were not yet accomplished, and among others that the Roman empire was not yet abolished . . .' The report spoken of by Moreau gained additional confirmation from the announcement made by an exorcised demoniac that in 1600 the Man of Sin had been born in the neighbourhood of Paris of a Jewess named Blanchefleure, who had been conceived by Satan. The child had been baptized at the Sabbath of Sorcerers; and a witch, under torture, acknowledged that she had rocked the infant Antichrist on her knees, and she averred that he had claws on his feet, wore no shoes, and spoke all languages.

In 1623 the brothers of the Order of St John of Jerusalem in the island of Malta reported that their spies in Babylon advised them that they had seen the infant Antichrist who had been born there on the 1 May of that year. They added that at his birth there appeared marvellous signs in heaven, including an eclipse of the sun, a swarm of flying serpents, and a shower of precious stones.

Babylon was then in the dominion of the Turks. But Antichrist was known to Muslims as well as to Christians. Lane, in his edition of the *Arabian Nights*, said that in the Muslim conception Antichrist will overrun the earth mounted on an ass and followed by 40,000 Jews. His empire will last forty days, but the first day will be a year long, the second a month, the third a week, and the others of usual length. He will devastate the whole world, leaving Mecca and Medina alone secure, as these holy cities will be guarded by angelic legions. Christ at last will descend to earth, and in a great battle will destroy the Man-devil.

Several writers, no less superstitious than the common people, connected the appearance of Antichrist with the fable of Pope Joan, which was widely believed at one time, but which modern criticism has at length succeeded in excluding from history.

The earliest writer *supposed* to mention Pope Joan is Anastatius the Librarian, who lived at the time of the alleged event and died in 886. Blondel, in his *Familier éclaircissement de la question, &c*, Amsterdam, 1647-1649, said he had seen the manuscript of Anastatius in the Royal Library at Paris and found that the story of Pope Joan was a later insertion using the words of Martinus Polonus, who lived 400 years afterwards and will be mentioned below. The next mention is in the chronicle of Marianus Scotus, a monk of Cologne and later of Metz who died in 1086. Where it does occur, this reference is specific: 'A.D. 854, Lotharii 14, [*i.e., in the 14th year of the reign of the Roman emperor Lothaire I*] Joanna, a woman, succeeded Leo, and reigned two years, five months and four days.' But in the manuscript copies of this chronicle the reference to Pope Joan is omitted in some, plainly asserted in others, and reported as hearsay in others – and it must be concluded that the passage is an insertion. The chronicler Sigebert de Gemblours, who died in 1112, is said to have referred to a Pope John VIII and to have added: 'It is reported that this John was a female and that she conceived by one of her servants. The Pope, becoming pregnant, gave birth to a child, wherefore some do not number her among the Pontiffs.' But there is direct evidence that later copies of this chronicle were tampered with, and the passage does not occur in the original Gemblours manuscript. The next commonly quoted authority is Martin Polonus (mentioned above) who died in 1279 and gave many circumstantial details of this supposed event, then four centuries old, styling her as John Anglus, a native of Metz, and providing most of the scandalous details which were later incorporated into the 'official' version propagated by the unscrupulous Protestant controversialists of the sixteenth century. This perfected version runs:

Joan was the daughter of an English missionary who left England to preach the gospel to the newly converted Saxons. She was born at Engelheim and was christened either Agnes or Gerberta or Joanna or Margaret or Isabel or Dorothy or Jutt. She early distinguished herself for genius and love of letters. A young monk of Fulda [*in the Rhineland*] having conceived for her a violent passion, which she returned with ardour, she deserted her parents, dressed herself in male attire, and in the sacred precincts of the Abbey of Fulda divided her affections between the youthful monk and the musty books of the monastic library. Not satisfied with the restraints of conventual life, nor finding the library sufficiently well provided with books of abstract science, she eloped with her young man, and after visiting England, France and Italy she brought him to Athens, where she addicted herself with unflagging devotion to her literary pursuits. Wearied out by his journey, the monk expired in the arms of the blue-stocking who had influenced his life for evil, and the young lady of so many aliases was for a while inconsolable. She left Athens and repaired to Rome. There she opened a school and acquired such a reputation for learning and feigned sanctity that, on the death of Leo IV, she was unanimously elected Pope. For two years and five months, under the name of John VIII, she filled the papal chair with reputation, no one suspecting her sex. But having taken a fancy to one of the cardinals, she became pregnant by him. The time of the Rogation processions arrived. Whilst passing the street between the amphitheatre and St Clement's, she was seized with violent pains, fell to the ground amidst the crowd, and whilst her attendants ministered to her she was delivered of a son. Some say the mother and child died on the spot, some that she survived but was incarcerated, some that the child was spirited away to be the Antichrist of the last days. A marble monument representing the papess with her baby was erected on the spot, which was declared to be accursed for all ages.

It need hardly be stated that the whole story of Pope Joan is fictitious and fabulous, and has not the slightest historical foundation. It was probably a Greek invention to throw discredit on the papal hierarchy, first circulated more than two hundred years after the date of the supposed Pope.

I have little doubt myself that Pope Joan is an impersonification of the great whore of the Revelation, seated on the seven hills, and is the popular expression of the idea prevalent from the twelfth to the sixteenth centuries that the mystery of iniquity was somehow working in the papal court. The scandal of the Antipopes, the utter worldliness and pride of others, the spiritual fornication with the kings of the earth, along with the words of Revelation prophesying the advent of an adulterous woman who should rule over the imperial city, and her connection with Antichrist, crystallized into this curious myth.

9.

The Man in the Moon

Everyone knows that the moon is inhabited by a man with a bundle of sticks on his back, who has been exiled there for many centuries, and who is so far off that he is beyond the reach of Death. He has once visited this earth, if the nursery rhyme is to be credited, when it asserts that:

> The Man in the Moon
> Came down too soon,
> And asked his way to Norwich.

But whether he ever reached that city, the authority does not state.

The story as told by nurses is that this man was found by Moses gathering sticks on a Sabbath, and that for this crime he was doomed to reside in the moon till the end of all things; and they refer to *Numbers*, xv, 32-36:

And while the children of Israel were in the wilderness they found a man that gathered sticks upon the sabbath day. And they that found him gathering sticks brought him unto Moses and Aaron and unto all the congregation. And they put him in ward, because it was not declared what should be done to him. And the Lord said unto Moses, The man shall surely be put to death: all the congregation shall stone him with stones without the camp. And all the congregation brought him without the camp, and stoned him with stones till he died.

Of course, in the sacred writings there is no allusion to the moon.

The German tale is as follows:

Ages ago there went one Sunday morning an old man into the wood to hew sticks. He cut a faggot and slung it on a stout staff, cast it over his shoulder, and began to trudge home with his burden. On his way he met a handsome man in a Sunday suit, walking towards the church. This man stopped and asked the faggot-bearer: 'Do you know that this is Sunday on earth, when all must rest from their labours?'

'Sunday on earth, or Monday in heaven, it is all the same to me,' laughed the wood-cutter.

'Then bear your bundle for ever,' answered the stranger. 'And as you do not value Sunday on earth, yours shall be a perpetual Moon-day in heaven; and you shall stand for eternity in the moon, a warn-ing to all Sabbath-breakers.' Thereupon the stranger vanished, and the man was caught up with his staff and his faggot into the moon, where he stands yet.

This tale is told with variations in many parts of Germany and Holland, and the notion of the man in the moon bearing a bundle of sticks is written in English manuscripts from the twelfth century. By Shakespeare's time the man had acquired a dog, and in the rustic play within *A Midsummer Night's Dream*, the rude mechanical who acts as Moonshine enters with the announcement 'All I have to say is to tell you that the lantern is the moon; I the man in the moon; this thorn-bush my thorn-bush; and this dog my dog.' In the *Tempest*, when Stephano the drunken butler assures Caliban that he was once the man in the moon, Caliban affirms: 'I have seen thee in her, and I do adore thee. My mistress showed me thee, and thy dog, and thy bush.'

Superstition in Devonshire puts a dog in the moon and a lamb in the sun, and it is said that those who see the sun rise on Easter Day can see within it the lamb and the flag. I believe this idea of locating animals in the sun and moon to be very ancient, a relic of a primeval superstition of the Aryan race. There is a curious seal appended to a deed preserved in the Record Office, dated the 9th year of Edward III (1335) showing the man in the moon with his sticks and dog and two stars.

In Scandinavian mythology Mâni, the moon, stole two children from their parents and carried them up to heaven. Their names were Hjuki and Bil. They had been drawing water from the well Byrgir, in the bucket Soegr, suspended from the pole Simul, which they bore on their shoulders. These children, pole and bucket, were placed in heaven 'where they could be seen from earth'. This refers undoubtedly to the spots on the moon, and so the Swedish peasantry explain these spots to this day as representing a boy and a girl bearing a pail of water between them. We are at once reminded of our nursery rhyme:

> Jack and Jill went up the hill
> To fetch a pail of water;
> Jack fell down and broke his crown,
> And Jill came tumbling after.

This verse, which to us at first sight seems nonsense, I have no hesitation in saying has a high antiquity, and refers to the Eddaic Hjuki and Bil. The names indicate as much. Hjuki, in Norse, would be pronounced Juki, which would readily become Jack; and Bil for the sake of euphony, and in order to give a female name to one of the children, would become Jill. The fall of Jack and the subsequent fall of Jill simply represent the vanishing of one moon-spot after another as the moon wanes.

But the old Norse myth had a deeper significance than merely an explanation of the moon-spots. Hjuki is derived from the verb jakka, to heap or pile together, to assemble and increase; and Bil from bila, to break up or dissolve. Hjuki and Bil therefore signify nothing more than the waxing and waning of the moon, and the water they are represented as bearing signifies the fact that the rainfall depends on the phases of the moon. Waxing and waning were individualized, and the meteorological fact of the connexion of the rain with the moon was represented by the children as water-bearers.

10.

The Mountain of Venus

RAGGED, BALD AND DESOLATE, as though a curse had rested upon it, rises the Hürselberg out of the rich and populous land between Eisenach and Gotha, looking from a distance like a huge stone sarcophagus – a sarcophagus in which rests, in magical slumber, till the end of all things, a mysterious world of wonders. High up on the north-west flank of the mountain, in a precipitous fall of rock, opens a cavern called the Hürseloch, from the depths of which issues a muffled roar of water, as though a subterranean stream were rushing over rapidly-whirling mill-wheels. In ancient days, according to the Thüringian Chronicles, bitter cries and long-drawn moans were heard issuing from this cavern; and at night wild shrieks and the burst of diabolical laughter would ring out from it over the vale, and fill the inhabitants with terror. It was supposed that this hole gave admittance to Purgatory and from it you could hear the cries of lost souls.

But another popular belief respecting this mountain was that in it Venus, the pagan goddess of love, held her court in all the pomp and revelry of heathendom; and there were not a few who declared that they had seen fair forms of female beauty beckoning them from the mouth of the chasm, and that they had heard dulcet strains of music well up from the abyss above the thunder of the falling, unseen torrent. Charmed by the music, and allured by the spectral forms, various individuals had entered the cave, and none had returned from this Venusberg except the Tannhäuser.

Tannhäuser, a French knight, was riding over the meadows in the

Hürsel vale on his way to the Wartburg, where the Landgrave
Hermann was holding a gathering of minstrels who were to contend
in song for a prize. Tannhäuser was a famous minnesinger, and all
his lays were of love and of women, for his heart was full of passion,
and that not of the purest and noblest description.

It was towards dusk that he passed the cliff in which is the Hürselloch, and as he rode by he saw a white glimmering figure of matchless
beauty standing before him and beckoning him to her. He knew her
at once, by her attributes and by her superhuman perfection, to be
none other than Venus. As she spoke to him the sweetest strains of
music floated in the air, a soft roseate light glowed around her,
and nymphs of exquisite loveliness scattered roses at her feet. A
thrill of passion ran through the veins of the minnesinger, and,
leaving his horse, he followed the apparition. It led him up the
mountain to the cave, and as it went flowers bloomed upon the soil
and a radiant track was left for Tannhäuser to follow. He entered
the cavern and descended to the palace of Venus in the heart of the
mountain.

Seven years of revelry and debauch were passed, and the minstrel's
heart began to feel a strange void. The beauty, the magnificence, the
variety of the scenes in the pagan goddess's home, and all its heath-
enish pleasures palled on him. He yearned for the pure, fresh breezes
of earth, one look up at the dark sky spangled with stars, one glimpse
of simple mountain flowers, one tinkle of sheep-bells. At the same
time his conscience began to reproach him, and he longed to make
his peace with God. In vain did he entreat Venus to permit him to
depart, and it was only when in the bitterness of his grief he called
upon the Virgin Mother that a rift in the mountain-side appeared
to him, and he stood again above ground.

How sweet was the morning, balmy with the scent of hay, as it
rolled up the mountain to him and fanned his haggard cheek! How
delightful to him was the cushion of moss and scanty grass after the
downy couches of the palace of revelry below! He plucked the little
heather-bells and held them before him. The tears rolled from his
eyes and moistened his thin and wasted hands. He looked up at the
soft blue sky and the newly-risen sun, and his heart overflowed. What
were the golden jewel-incrusted, lamplit vaults beneath compared
to that pure dome of God's building!

The chime of the village church struck sweetly on his ear, satiated
with Bacchanalian songs. He hurried down to the valley church

which had called him. There he made his confession, but the priest, horror-struck at his recital, dared not give him absolution but passed him on to another. And so he went on from one to another till at last he was referred to the Pope himself. To the Pope he went. Urban IV then occupied the chair of St Peter. To him Tannhäuser related the sickening story of his guilt, and prayed for absolution. Urban was a hard and stern man, and, shocked at the immensity of the sin, he thrust the penitent indignantly from him, exclaiming 'Guilt such as thine can never, never be remitted. Sooner shall this staff in my hand grow green and blossom than that God should pardon thee!'

Then Tannhäuser, full of despair and with his soul darkened, went away and returned to the only asylum open to him, the Venusberg. But lo! three days after he had gone, Urban discovered that his pastoral staff had put forth buds and had burst into flower. Then he sent messengers after Tannhäuser, and they reached the Hürsel vale to hear that a wayworn man, with haggard brow and bowed head, had just entered the Hürselloch. Since then the Tannhäuser has not been seen.

The story of Tannhäuser is a very ancient myth Christianized, a widespread tradition localized, existing in various forms scattered over Europe – and indeed there are at least three other Venusbergs in Germany. The root of all forms of the story is this:

The underground folk seek union with human beings. (1) A man is enticed into their abode, where he unites with a woman of the underground race. (2) He desires to revisit the earth, and escapes. (3) He returns to the region below.

There is scarcely a collection of folk-lore which does not contain a story founded on this root. It appears in every branch of the Aryan family, and examples could be quoted from Modern Greek, Albanian, Neapolitan, French, German, Danish, Norwegian and Swedish, Icelandic, Scots, Welsh and other collections of popular tales.

The Scots story is of Thomas of Ercildoune, who met a strange lady of elfin race beneath Eildon Tree. She led him into the underground land, where he remained with her for seven years. He then returned to earth, still, however, bound to come to his royal mistress whenever she should summon him. Accordingly, while Thomas was making merry with his friends in the Tower of Ercildoune, a person came running in and told with marks of fear and astonishment that a hart and a hind had left the neighbouring forest and were parading in the street of the village. Thomas instantly arose, left his house, and followed the animals into the forest, from which he never returned. According to popular belief he still 'drees his weird' in Fairy Land, and is one day expected to revisit earth. (Scott, *Minstrelsy of the Scottish Border*.)

Unquestionably the Venus of the Hürselberg, of the Eildon Hill and of so many other locations all over Europe is the ancient goddess Holda, or Thorgerda. But the legend as it shaped itself in the Middle Ages is indicative of the struggle between the new and the old faith. We see thinly veiled in Tannhäuser the story of a man, Christian in name but heathen at heart, allured by the attractions of Paganism, which seems to satisfy his poetic instincts and gives full rein to his passions. But these excesses pall on him after a while, and the religion of sensuality leaves a great void in his breast.

He turns to Christianity, and at first it seems to promise all that he requires. But alas! he is repelled by its ministers. On all sides he is met by practice widely at variance with profession. Pride, worldliness, want of sympathy, exist among those who should be the foremost to guide, sustain and receive him. All the warm springs which gushed up into his broken heart are choked, his softened spirit is hardened again, and he returns in despair to bury his sorrows and drown his anxieties in the debauchery of his former creed.

A sad picture, but doubtless one very true.

11.

St Patrick's Purgatory

IN A CHARMING mediaeval romance, *Fortunatus and his Sons*, there is an account of a visit paid by that favoured youth to the cave of mystery in Lough Derg, the Purgatory of Saint Patrick. Fortunatus, we are told, had heard in his travels of how two days' journey from a town Valdric in Iceland was the town Vernic where there was the entrance to the Purgatory, so he went there with many servants. He found a great abbey, and behind the altar of the church, a door which led into the dark cave which is called the Purgatory of St Patrick. In order to enter it, leave had to be obtained from the abbot. Consequently a servant of Fortunatus went to the abbot and told him that a nobleman from Cyprus desired to enter the mysterious cavern. The abbot requested the company of Fortunatus at supper, and the nobleman sent a large jar of wine as a present to the monastery. At supper he asked the abbot: 'Venerable sir, I understand that the Purgatory of Saint Patrick is here. Is it so?'

The abbot replied:

It is so indeed. Many hundred years ago this place where the abbey and the town now stand was a howling wilderness. Not far off, however, lived a venerable hermit, Patrick by name, who was exposing himself to the desert for self-discipline one day when he came across this vast cave. He went in, wandered on in the dark, and lost his way, so that he had no idea of how he should return to the light of day. After long ramblings through the gloomy passages he fell on his knees and besought Almighty God, if it were His will, to deliver him from the great peril in which he lay. Whilst Patrick thus prayed he was aware of piteous cries issuing from the depths of the cave, just such as would be the wailings of souls in purgatory. The hermit rose from his orison and by God's mercy found his way back to the surface. From that day he exercised greater austerities of self-discipline, and after his death he was numbered with the saints. Pious people who had heard the story of Patrick's adventure in the cave built this cloister on the site.

Then Fortunatus asked whether all who ventured into the place heard in the same way the howls of the tormented souls.

The abbot replied, 'Some have affirmed that they have heard a bitter crying and piping therein, whilst others have heard and seen nothing. No one, however, has penetrated as yet to the furthest limits of the cavern.'

Fortunatus then asked permission to enter, and the abbot cheerfully consented, only stipulating that his guest should keep near the entrance and not ramble too far, as some who had ventured in had never returned.

Early next day Fortunatus received the Blessed Sacrament with his trusty servant Leopold. The door of the Purgatory was unlocked. Each was provided with a taper. Then, with the blessing of the abbot, they were left in total darkness and the door was bolted behind them. Both wandered on in the cave, hearing faintly the chanting of the monks in the church, till the sound died away. They traversed several passages, lost their way, their candles burnt out and they sat down in despair on the ground, a prey to hunger, thirst and fear.

The monks waited in the church hour after hour, and the visitors to Purgatory had not returned. Day declined, vespers were sung, and still there was no sign of the two who in the morning had passed from the church into the cave. Then the servants of Fortunatus began to demonstrate anger and insist on their master being restored to them. The abbot was frightened, and sent for an old man who had once penetrated far into the cave with a ball of twine, the end attached to a door handle. This man volunteered to seek Fortunatus, and providentially his search was successful. After this the abbot refused permission to any one to visit the cave.

In the reign of Henry II, Henry of Saltrey wrote a history of the visit of a Knight Owen to the Purgatory of St Patrick which gained immense popularity (*Biograph Brit. Lit.; Anglo-Norm. Period.* p. 321). This account was soon translated into other languages, and spread the fable through mediaeval Europe. Marie of France turned the tale into French metre, but hers was not the only version in that tongue, and nor indeed was Henry of Saltrey's (*Owayne Miles*, H. S. Cotton. Calig. A ii, fol. 89). The myth has been exhaustively treated by Thomas Wright (*St Patrick's Purgatory*, London, 1844.)

Unquestionably the story is founded on the ancient Hell-descents prevalent in all heathen nations: Herakles, Orpheus, Odysseus in Greek mythology, Aeneas in Roman, descend to the nether world and behold sights very similar to those described in the Christian legends which were built around the cave of Lough Derg. Norse, Finn and Esthonian legend include similar features. Among the Greeks a descent into the cave of Trophonius occupied much the same place in their popular mysticism that the Purgatory of St Patrick assumed among Christians. The myth of St Patrick's Purgatory originated among the Celts, and in ancient Celtic mythology the nether world was divided into three circles corresponding with Purgatory, Hell and Heaven; and over our Hell was cast a bridge, very narrow, which souls were obliged to cross if they hoped to reach the mansions of light.

12.

The Terrestrial Paradise

THE EXACT POSITION of the earthly paradise of Eden, and its present condition, does not seem to have occupied the minds of our Anglo-Saxon ancestors, nor to have given rise among them to wild speculations. The tenth-century map in the British Museum accompanying the Periegesis of Priscian is far more correct than the generality of maps which we find in manuscripts at a later period; and Paradise does not occupy the place of Cochin China or the isles of Japan, as it did later after the fabulous voyage of St Brandan had become popular in the eleventh century. [*Brandan, an Irish monk living at the close of the sixth century, chronicled an alleged voyage of exploration which is full of absurdities and seems to be founded on the feats of Sinbad the sailor. It has been republished by Jubinal from manuscripts in the Bibliothéque du Roi, Paris, 1836. The earliest printed English edition is that of Wynkyn de Worde, London, 1516.*] The site of Eden has been indicated by Cosmas, who wrote in the seventh century and specified it as occupying a continent east of China, beyond the ocean, and still watered by the four great rivers Pison, Gihon, Hiddekel and Euphrates, which sprang from subterranean canals. In a map of the ninth century preserved in the Strasbourg Library the terrestrial Paradise is placed at the extreme east of Asia, in China, and it occupies the same position in a Turin manuscript and also in a map accompanying a commentary on the Apocalypse in the British Museum.

According to the fictitious letter of Prester John to the Emperor Emanuel Comnenus, already quoted in this work, Paradise was situated within three days' journey of his own territories, but where those lands lay is not distinctly specified. But he mentions a mountain called Olympus within his domains, as the source of the fountain which varied in taste hour by hour. This is undoubtedly Alumbo, Polombe, or modern Colombo in Ceylon, where Sir John Mandeville found at the foot of Mount Polombe:

... a fair great well that hath odour and savour of all spices, and at every hour of the day he changeth his odour and his savour diversely: and whoso drinketh three times fasting of the water of that well, he is whole of all manner of sickness that he hath. And they that dwell there and drink often of that well, they never have sickness and they seem always young. I have drunk there three or four times, and methinks I am better already. Some men call it the Well of Youth, for they that drink thereat often seem always young and live without sickness. And men say that the well comes out of Paradise, and therefore it is so virtuous.

In the twelfth and thirteenth centuries Paradise began to assume a place in an unapproachable region of Asia, inaccessible because of a wall of fire surrounding it, and having an armed angel to guard the only gate. Paludanus related in his *Thesaurus Novus* that Alexander the Great was so full of desire to see the terrestrial Paradise that he undertook his wars in the East for the express purpose of reaching it and obtaining admission to it. He states that on the monarch's near approach to Eden an old man was captured in a ravine by some of Alexander's soldiers and they were about to conduct him to the king when the venerable man said: 'Go and announce to Alexander that it is in vain he seeks Paradise. His efforts will be perfectly fruitless, for the way of Paradise is the way of humility, a way of which he knows nothing. Take this stone and give it to Alexander, and say to him: "From this stone learn what you must think of yourself." Now this stone was of great value and excessively heavy, outweighing and excelling in value all other gems, but when reduced to powder it was as light as a tuft of hay, and as worthless. By which token the mysterious old man meant that Alexander alive was the greatest of monarchs, but Alexander dead would be a thing of nought.

The mediaeval preacher Meffreth claimed St Basil and St Ambrose as his authorities for placing Paradise on the top of a very lofty mountain in eastern Asia, where its elevation enabled it to escape the Flood. A manuscript in the British Museum alleges that it escaped the Flood because it is suspended between heaven and earth, forty fathoms higher than the highest hills, and goes on to give a very attractive circumstantial description of the place. St Brandan had been incited to go to Paradise by a monk who had already spent a six-month stay there after sailing due east of Ireland, and somehow missing Wales, and on the monk's return to the abbey his garments were still fragrant with the odours of Paradise. Brandan eventually reached the same island and spent forty days there without meeting anyone until he came to a river which divided the world into two, and a solitary angel informed him that no one living might pass it.

In general all the mediaeval authorities placed Paradise beyond India – either farther east or in Ceylon. The subject was not abandoned after the Renaissance, and later work on the subject has been done by G. C. Kirchmayer, *De Paradiso*, Wittemberg, 1662; Carver, *Discourse on the Terrestrian Paradise*, 1666; Père Hardouin, *Nouveau Traité de la Situation du Paradis Terrestre*, La Haye, 1730; and a paper by Sir W. Ouseley on the situation of Eden, read before the Literary Society of London in 1842.

13.

Saint George

THE LEGENDS ATTACHED to this celebrated soldier-martyr contain, almost unaltered, representative myths of the Semitic and Aryan peoples which can be traced to their respective roots. The popular traditions concerning him are sacred myths of faded creeds absorbed into a newer faith and re-coloured. St George has been generally supposed to be the un-named martyr mentioned by Eusebius (*Eccl. Hist.* viii, c. 5) who publicly tore to pieces an edict of the Emperor Diocletian [*ruled the east and west empires A.D. 285-313*] against the Christian churches in Nicomedia [*modern Izmit, Turkey, on the Sea of Marmora: as Nicomedia, was the seat of the emperors Diocletian and Constantine.*]

This protester, a responsible soldier, was immediately executed and the date can be fixed with some certainty as A.D. 303 in Nicomedia. His popularity as a saint grew with astonishing speed. Veneration for him quickly extended through Phoenicia, Palestine and the whole East. A Greek inscription naming St George as a holy martyr dated A.D. 346 has been found in an ancient church at Ezra, Syria (*Transactions of the Royal Society of Literature*, 2nd series, vol vii, pt i, article by Hogg) : and this is a most valuable discovery protecting the martyr of 303 from being confused, as he often was previously, with the George who was a tyrannical Bishop of Alexandria and was finally put to death after an uprising of his own people. Gibbon made this confusion, and therefore wasted a keen passage of irony when he wrote: 'The odious stranger, disguising every circumstance of time and place, assumed the mask of a martyr, a saint and a Christian hero; and the infamous George of Cappadocia has been transformed into the renowned Saint George of England, the patron of arms, of chivalry, and of the Garter.' (*Decline and Fall*, Chap. XXIII). Both Georges did indeed come from Cappadocia: the martyr was born there and the bishop had fled there after certain fraudulent deeds of his had been discovered in Constantinople. But the bishop was still alive in A.D. 346 when the church inscription to the martyr of the year 303 was carved, and the second George was not executed until 362.

I am disposed to believe that there really was such a person as St George, that he was a martyr to the Catholic faith, and that the very uncertainty which existed regarding him tended to give the composers of his biography the opportunity of attaching to him popular heathen myths which had been floating, unadopted by any Christian hero. The number of warrior saints was not so very great; Sebastian's history was fixed, so were those of Maurice and Gereon, but George was unprovided with a history. The deficiency was soon supplied. By the fifth century he was being honoured in Gaul. In the sixth century the earliest extant annals concerning him were written. In the seventh century he already had two churches in Rome.

The Greek chronicles are fabulous, since they were written long after the event of his death, which had made a very deep impact at the time but had given rise to little strong or reliable oral tradition about him. The Greek documents said:

George was born of Christian parents in Cappadocia *north-east Asia Minor*]. His father suffered a martyr's death, and the mother with her child took refuge in Palestine. He early entered the army, and behaved with great courage and endurance. At the age of twenty he was bereaved of his mother, and by her death came in for a large fortune. He then went to the court of Diocletian, where he hoped to find advancement. On the breaking out of the persecution he distributed his money among the poor and declared himself, before the Emperor, to be a Christian. Having been ordered to sacrifice, he refused and was condemned to death. On the first day he was thrust with spears to prison, and one of the spears snapped like straw when it touched him. He was then fastened by the feet and hands to posts, and a heavy stone was laid upon his breast.

On the second day he was bound to a wheel set with swords and knife-blades. Diocletian believed him to be dead. But an angel appeared and George courteously saluted him in military fashion, and by this the persecutor ascertained that the saint was still living. On removing him from the wheel, it was discovered that all his wounds were healed. George was then cast into a pit of quick-lime, which however did not cause his death. On the next day but one the Emperor sent to have his limbs broken, and he was discovered on his knees, perfectly whole.

He was next made to run in red-hot iron shoes. The following night and day he spent in prayer, and on the sixth day he appeared before Diocletian walking and unhurt. He was then scourged with thongs of hide till his flesh came off his back, but he was well next day.

On the seventh day he drank two cups, one of which was intended to make him mad and the other to poison him. He experienced no ill effects. He then performed some miracles, raised a dead man to life, and restored to life an ox which had been killed. These miracles resulted in numerous conversions.

That night, George dreamed that the Saviour laid a golden crown on his head and bade him prepare for Paradise. St George at once called to him the servant 'who has written these memoirs' [*this is the actual claim made in the original Greek chronicle*] and commanded him, after his death, to take his body and will to Palestine. On the eighth day the saint, by the force of the sign of the cross, compelled the devil inhabiting the statue of Apollo to declare that he was a fallen angel; then all the statues of the gods fell before him.

This miracle converted the Empress Alexandra, and Diocletian was so exasperated against the truth that he condemned her to instant death. George was then executed. The day of his martyrdom was 23 April.

A second posthumous chronicle of George is extant in Latin, but is a translation of a Greek original (now missing) differing from the sixth-century account which has been summarised. The Latin manuscript records:

The devil urged Dacian, Emperor of the Persians, king of the four quarters of heaven, having dominion over seventy-two kings, to persecute the Church. At this time lived George of Cappadocia, a native of Melitena, and Melitena, where he lived with a holy widow, is the scene of his martyrdom. He was subjected to numerous tortures, such as the rack, iron pincers, fire, a sword-spiked wheel, shoes nailed to his feet; he was put into an iron box set within with sharp nails, and flung down a precipice; he was beaten with sledge-hammers, a pillar

was laid on him, a heavy stone dashed on to his head; he was stretched on a red-hot iron bed, melted lead was poured over him; he was
cast into a well, transfixed with forty long nails, shut into a brazen
bull over a fire, and cast into a well with a stone around his neck.
Each time he returned from a torment he was restored to his former
vigour. His tortures continued through seven years. His constancy
and miracles were the means of converting 40,900 men, and the
Empress Alexandra. Dacian then ordered the execution of George
and his queen; and as they died a whirlwind of fire carried off the
persecutor.

These two records are the source of all the later legends, though
the gory imagination of those who embellished the tale in the middle
ages added the characteristically sadistic tortures which fascinated
them perhaps more than the old traditional agony. But the main
feature of this Oriental Christian story did not change. St George
suffered at least seven martyrdoms, and revived after each one except
the last.

The Muslims revere St George equally with the Christians. Their
account of him is basically the same. Gherghis, or El Khoudi, as he is
called by them, lived at the same time as the Prophet. He was sent
by God to the king of El Mauçil with the command that he should
accept the faith. This the king refused to do, and ordered the execution of Gherghis. The saint was slain, but God revived him, and sent
him to the king again. A second time he was slain, and again God
restored him to life. A third time he preached his mission. Then the
persecutor had him burned, and his ashes scattered in the Tigris. But
God restored him to life once more, and destroyed the king and all
his subjects. The Greek historian John Kantakuzenos who died in
1380 reported that there were then several shrines erected to the
memory of St George at which the Mohammedans paid their devo-
tions, and the traveller Burckmann recorded 'the Turks pay great
veneration to St George'. Dean Stanley (*Sinai and Palestine*, p. 274)
saw a Muslim chapel dedicated to El Khoudi on the sea-shore near
Sarafend and noted: 'There is no tomb inside, only hangings before
a recess. This variation from the usual type of Mussulman sepulchres
was, as we were told by peasants on the spot, because El Khoudi is
not yet dead, but flies round and round the world, and these chapels
are built wherever he has appeared.'

Another civilisation, that of the Nabathae, who for two centuries
before Christ dominated the stretch between the Red Sea and the

Mediterranean from their rose-red capital of Petra, had a hero called Tammuz, a prophet who was cruelly put to death several times, but revived after each martyrdom. When the festival of his eventual death came round each year at high summer it was an occasion for deep mourning and frenzied wailing. But, curiously, the time of year when Tammuz was supposed to have died was the depth of winter.

The Phoenicians had a god identical with Tammuz whom they called Adonis. This name is purely Semitic and signifies 'the Lord'. The Phoenicians introduced his worship to the Greeks by way of Crete. Adonis was identified with the sun. The Greek myth said that Aphrodite, the goddess of love, became so enamoured of him that the jealousy of the god Ares was aroused, and Ares arranged that Adonis should be killed by a wild boar. But when Adonis descended into the shades, Persephone, the goddess of the underworld fell deeply in love with him. There was therefore a fresh jealousy, between Aphrodite and Persephone, which Zeus resolved by allowing Adonis to spend six months in the heavens with Aphrodite and six months in the land of gloom with Persephone. Among the Greeks the celebration of the festival of Adonis is accompanied by mourning and wailing, seeking and finding.

The Syrians had a god, Baal, who was identical with the Phoenician Adonis. The Egyptians had a glorious god and hero, Osiris, who was killed by an evil god and passed half his time in heaven and half in the lower world, his festival being accompanied by wailing and a formula of seeking and finding. The Arabs had their prophet El Khoudi, previously called Ta'z and later called Ghenghis, who had been killed several times by a wicked king and who revived each time. And the Oriental Christians had their saint, George, a soldier killed by a wicked king who underwent numerous torments but revived each time. On earth he lived with a widow. He took to the other world with him a queen. His festival celebration discarded wailing, seeking and finding, and was solely one of revivification through commemoration.

From this tabulation it is, I think, impossible not to see that St George is in his mythical character a Semitic god Christianized. In order to undergo the process of conversion, a few little arrangements were necessary – to divest the story of its sensuous character and to purify it. Aphrodite had to be got out of the way, and she was made into a pious widow in whose house the youthful saint lodged. Persephone, the queen of Hades had to be accounted for, and she was turned into the martyr Alexandra who accompanied George as queen to the unseen world. Consequently, in the land of light George was with the widow, in the land of gloom with Alexandra. George was the personification of the sun, which not only seems to die each night, but more convincingly seems to die each winter – yet, after mourning, he is sought and he finally re-appears. The manner in which St George dies repeatedly represents the different ways in which the sun dies at the end of day.

So much for the Eastern myth of St George, as shaped by the Oriental Christians. The Western myth makes much of his fight with the dragon. The story of St George and the dragon first presents itself in the *Legenda Aurea* of Jacques de Voragine and was so unquestioningly accepted by priests and laity in the middle ages that the dragon received its due mention in the office-books of the Church, and clerks using the Sarum Missal sang (in Latin) on St George's Day of the 'royal maiden saved from the fearful dragon' until Pope Clement VII cut out the reference when he revised the missals and breviaries in the Reformation following Henry VIII's breach with the papacy. The golden legend of Jacques de Voragine runs:

George, a tribune, was born in Cappadocia, and came to Lybia, to the town called Silene, near which was a pond infested by a monster which had many times driven back an armed host that had come to destroy him. He even approached the walls of the city, and with his exhalations poisoned all who were near. To avoid such visits, he was furnished with two sheep each day to satisfy his voracity. If these were not given, he attacked the walls of the town so that his envenomed breath infected the air and many of the inhabitants died. He was supplied with sheep until they were exhausted and it was impossible to procure the necessary number. Then the citizens held counsel, and it was decided that each day a man and a beast should be offered, so that at last they gave up their children, sons and daughters, and none were spared. The lot fell one day on the princess. The monarch, horror-struck, offered in exchange for her his gold, his silver and half his realm, only desiring to save his daughter from this frightful death. But the people insisted on the sacrifice of the maiden, and all the poor father could obtain was a delay of eight days in which to bewail the fate of the damsel.

At the expiration of this time the people returned to the palace and said 'Why do you sacrifice your subjects for your daughter? We are all dying before the breath of this monster!' The king felt that he must resolve on parting with his child. He covered her with royal clothes, embraced her and said: 'Alas! dear daughter, I thought to have seen myself re-born in your offspring. I hoped to have invited princes to your wedding, to have adorned you with royal garments, and accompanied you with flutes, tambourins and all kinds of music; but you are to be devoured by this monster! Why did I not die before you?'

Then she fell at her father's feet and besought his blessing. He accorded it to her, weeping and clasping her tenderly in his arms. Then she went to the lake. George, who passed that way, saw her weeping and asked the cause of her tears. She replied: 'Good youth, quickly mount your horse and fly, lest you perish with me!' But George said to her: 'Do not fear. Tell me what you await and why all this multitude look on.' She answered: 'I see that you have a pure and noble heart, yet fly!' 'I shall not go without knowing the cause,' he replied. Then she explained all to him. Whereupon he exclaimed: 'Fear nothing. In the name of Jesus Christ I will assist you.' 'Brave knight,' she said, 'do not seek to die with me. Enough that I should perish, for you can neither assist nor deliver me, and you will only die with me.'

At this moment the monster rose above the surface of the water. And the virgin said, all trembling, 'Fly, fly, sir knight!' His only answer was the sign of the cross. Then he advanced to meet the monster, recommending himself to God.

He brandished his lance with such force that he transfixed the dragon and cast it to the ground. Then he bade the princess pass her girdle around it and fear nothing. When this was done the monster followed like a docile hound. When they brought it to the town the people fled before it. But George called them back, bidding them put aside all fear, for the Lord had sent him to deliver them from the dragon. Then the king and all his people, twenty thousand men without counting the women and children, were baptized, and George smote off the head of the monster.

There are other versions of the story, and it has been attached to other saints and heroes of the middle ages. It is essentially the same as the myth of Perseus and Andromeda and many other legends of ancient Greece, and they are all echoes of the principal myth of Apollo and Python. Similar myths are found among the Scandinavian and Teutonic peoples, where Apollo is replaced by Sigurd, Siegfried and Beowulf. In Indian and Iranian mythology the same story occurs. The fight with the dragon is a myth common to all Aryan peoples. Its significance is that the maiden whom the dragon attempts to devour is the earth. The monster is the storm-cloud. The hero who fights it is the sun, with his glorious sword, the lightning-flash. By his victory the earth is relieved from her peril. And when we perceive how popular this venerable myth was in heathen nations of Europe it is not surprising that it should perpetuate itself under Christianity and that, when once transferred to a hero of a new creed, it should make that hero one of the most venerated and popular of all the saints in the calendar.

In the reign of Constantine the Great there was a great and beautiful church between Arimathaea and Lydda (both of which towns claimed to be the birthplace of the saint) dedicated by the Emperor to St George and enclosing his tomb. Later the bones were conveyed from this tomb to a church in Constantinople. His head was taken to Rome and was rediscovered there in A.D. 751 with an inscription on the casket which identified it with St George: it was given to a church in Ferrara in 1600. Churches and convents were dedicated to St George all over Christendom, and in Thetford he had his own monastery founded in the reign of King Canute. A collegiate church in Oxford was placed under his invocation in the reign of the Conqueror, and St George's in Southwark dates from before that time. The Crusades gave an impetus to the veneration of the patron, and the enthusiasm of the Crusaders for the Eastern soldier-saint who led them to battle soon raised St George to the highest pitch of popularity among the nobles and fighting men of Europe. England, Aragon and Portugal assumed him as their patron, as well as most chivalrous orders founded at the time of these wars. In 1245 on St George's Day Frederic of Austria instituted an order of knighthood under his patronage, and its banner, white charged with a blood-red cross, floated in battle alongside that of the empire. In 1348 King Edward III founded St George's Chapel, Windsor, and with it the order of the Garter, now and for long time past the most ancient order of chivalry in the world. In 1349 the king was besieging Calais. Moved by a sudden impulse, says Thomas of Walsingham, he drew his sword with the cry: 'Ha! Saint Edward! Ha! Saint George!' The words and action instilled spirit in his soldiers and they fell with vigour on the French and routed them. From that time St George replaced Edward the Confessor as patron of England. In 1415, by the Constitutions of Archbishop Chichely, St George's Day was made a major double feast and ordered to be observed the same as Christmas Day, all labour ceasing; and he received the title of spiritual patron of the English soldiery. Since the time of Henry VIII, with one short gap under Edward VI, the meeting of the chapter of the Garter is held annually on the feast of the patron of the order, Saint George.

Beneath the Western fable there lies a graceful allegory. St George is any Christian who is sealed at his baptism to be 'Christ's faithful soldier and servant unto his life's end,' and armed with the breastplate of righteousness, the shield of the faith marked with its bloodred cross, the helmet of salvation and the sword of the Spirit, which is the word or power of God. The hideous monster against whom the Christian soldier is called to fight is that 'old serpent, the devil,' who withholds or poisons the streams of grace, and who seeks to rend or devour the virgin soul, in whose defence the champion fights.

14.

St Ursula and the Eleven Thousand Virgins

THE FABLE OF ST URSULA is too important to be omitted from this collection of myths, because of the extravagance of its details, the devotion which it excited, the persistency with which the Church clings to it, and because it is a specimen of the manner in which saintly legends were developed in the Middle Ages, sometimes generated out of worse than nothing. Ursula and the eleven thousand British virgins are said to have suffered martyrdom at Cologne on 21 October, A.D. 237. But since they are supposed to have suffered under the Huns on their return from the defeat by Aëtius at Chalons, and this event occured in 451, the anachronism is considerable. There is no mention of Ursula, let alone her eleven thousand maiden companions, in any martyrology before the tenth century, when there occurs a reference to St Hilario and eleven thousand virgins. By the year 1100 there seems to occur in the chronicle of Sigebert of Gemblours – but, as in an earlier reference to this manuscript history, there are signs that a later interpolation has been stitched into the parchment – a detailed story, under the date 453, of the Virgin Ursula, daughter of a wealthy British prince Nothus, who was sought in marriage by a ferocious tyrant though she had dedicated herself to celibacy. To evade the obligation she persuaded her father to agree a contract of marriage with the tyrant provided that ten other beautiful virgins should be chosen, they should each be given a thousand damsels under them, and that they should be allowed to embark on eleven triremes and cruise the world for three years in unsullied virginity. Ursula had hoped that this would prove an impossible condition, but the tyrant energetically mustered the eleven thousand virgins and eleven elegantly furnished galleys. For three years they sailed the seas. One day the wind blew them into the port of Tiela in Gaul, and thence up the Rhine to Cologne and on to Basle. They left their ships and crossed the Alps on foot, reached Rome and visited the tombs of the Apostles, and returned to the Rhine. But on reaching Cologne again, they fell in with the Huns and were all martyred by the barbarians. This story, once written, found its way into many later chronicles, including that of Geoffrey of Monmouth in 1154, though Geoffrey varied the details.

In 1106 Cologne had been besieged and the walls battered down. During rebuilding the citizens excavated fresh foundations, which happened to be on the site of the ancient cemetery of the historic Roman settlement of Colonia Agrippina. A large number of bones were discovered, and it was conveyed in a vision to a willing recipient that these were the bones of the eleven thousand virgins. But in the midst of the consequent religious enthusiasm it was evident that a number of the bones belonged to men, which was disconcerting to any belief in the virgins' purity. A second convenient vision gave the assurance that Pope Cyriacus and a number of cardinals of Rome, with bishops, priests and monks, had been so impressed by the visit of the virgins that they had accompanied them back to Cologne, on a strictly celibate understanding, and that they too had been massacred by the Huns. But further excavations disclosed a number of children's bones, some belonging to infants only a few months old. Scandal and ridicule rose again, complicated by the fact that the nun who had received the earlier visions was now dead. Fortunately an old English monk named Richard living in the abbey of Arnsberg in the diocese of Cologne volunteered for celestial communication and was assured in another vision that the eleven thousand virgins had excited such enthusiasm in England that their married relations had accompanied them in the galleys and on to Rome, and they with their children had also received the martyr's crown. Honour was re-established, and to this day the church of St Ursula in Cologne is visited by thousands who rely on the intercession of a saint who never existed, and believe in the miraculous virtues of relics which are those pagans.

Ursula is in fact none other than the Swabian goddess Ursel or Hörsel (Hürsel) to whom human sacrifices were occasionally made and who became the Venus of the Venusberg, or Hürselberg, who entranced and debauched Tannhäuser.

15.

The Legend of the Cross

THE CROSS WAS A sacred sign among the Gaulish Celts, and they inscribed a cross in the middle of their most sacred coins. The shamrock of Ireland derives its sacredness because it approaches the same form. In the mysticism of the Druids the stalk or long arm of the cross represented the way of life and the three lobes of the clover-leaf, or the short arms of the cross, symbolized the three conditions of the spirit-world, Heaven, Purgatory and Hell. To the Scandinavians Thor was the thunder and the hammer was his symbol. This hammer was a cross, the cross cramponnée which appeared on Scandinavian coins and is still used as a magical sign in Iceland. This cross is the sacred Swastika of the Buddhist [*not the Nazi swastika, which is in fact the cross cramponnée reversed*] and the same sign occurs on coins of ancient Syracuse, Corinth and Chalcedon and on Etruscan urns. A form of the cross symbolized The Life to Come to the Egyptians and was the symbol of their god Serapis: it is now known as the *ankh* or *crux ansata* and was adopted by the early Christians for a time. In ancient Nineveh the kings wore the Maltese cross on their breast. Long before the Romans and even before the Etruscans, there lived a primitive people in northern Italy to whom the cross was a religious symbol, the sign beneath which they laid their dead to rest. In the Inca and 'Indian' civilisations of central and south America the cross was honoured as a sacred symbol and mothers placed new-born children under that sign because it was believed to have the power to drive away evil sprits. The Hebrews used the T-shaped cross as a sign, and St Jerome, who knew the Hebrew tongue well, averred that this was the mark referred to in *Ezekiel* ix 4-6 as a mark of salvation:

The Lord said unto him, Go through the midst of the city, through the midst of Jerusalem, and set a mark upon the foreheads of the men that sigh and that cry for all the abominations that be done in the midst thereof. Slay utterly old and young, both maids and little children, and women: but come not near any man on whom is the mark; and begin at My sanctuary.

But in the Middle Ages people wanted to see the cross still more strongly characterized in the history of the Jewish Church, and as the records of the Old Testament were deficient on that point, they supplemented them with fable. That fable is the Legend of the Cross, a romance of immense popularity in the Middle Ages, told in full in the *Vita Christi* printed at Troyes in 1517, in the *Legenda Aurea* of Jacques de Voragine, in an old Dutch work, *Gerschiedenis van det heylighe Cruys*, and in a thirteenth-century manuscript in the British Museum. The story is as follows:

When Adam was banished from Paradise he lived in penitence, striving to recompense for the past by prayer and toil. When he reached a great age and felt death approach, he summoned Seth to his side and said: 'Go, my son, to the earthly Paradise and ask the Archangel who keeps the gate to give me a balsam which will save me from death. You will easily find the way, because my footprints scorched the soil as I left Paradise. Follow my blackened traces, and they will conduct you to the gate where I was expelled.' Seth hastened to Paradise. The way was barren, vegetation was scanty and of sombre colours; over all lay the black prints of his father's and mother's feet. Presently the walls surrounding Paradise appeared. Around them nature revived, the earth was covered with verdure and dappled with flowers. The air vibrated with exquisite music. Seth was dazzled with the beauty which surrounded him, and he walked on forgetful of his mission. Suddenly there flashed before him a wavering line of fire, upright, like a serpent of light continuously quivering. It was the flaming sword in the hand of the Cherub who guarded the gate. As Seth drew near he saw that the angel's wings were expanded so as to block the door. He prostrated himself before the Cherub, unable to utter a word. But the celestial being read in his soul, better than a mortal can read a book, the words which were there impressed, and he said: 'The time of pardon is not yet come. Four thousand years must roll away ere the Redeemer shall open the gate to Adam, closed by his disobedience. But as a token of future pardon, the wood whereon redemption shall be won shall grow from the tomb of thy father. Behold what he lost by his transgression!'

At these words the angel swung open the great portal of gold and fire, and Seth looked in.

He beheld a fountain, clear as crystal, sparkling like silver dust, playing in the midst of the garden, and gushing forth in four living streams. Before this mystic fountain grew a mighty tree, with a trunk of vast bulk, and thickly branched, but destitute of bark and foliage. Around the bole was wreathed a frightful serpent or caterpillar, which had scorched the bark and devoured the leaves. Beneath the tree was a precipice. Seth beheld the roots of the tree in Hell. There Cain was endeavouring to grasp the roots, and clamber up them into Paradise. But they laced themselves around the body and limbs of the fratricide, as the threads of a spider's web entangle a fly, and the fibres of the tree penetrated the body of Cain as though they were endued with life.

Horror-struck at this appalling spectacle, Seth raised his eyes to the summit of the tree. Now all was changed. The tree had grown till its branches reached heaven. The boughs were covered with leaves, flowers and fruit. But the fairest fruit was a little babe, a living sun, who seemed to be listening to the songs of seven white doves who circled round his head. A woman, more lovely than the moon, bore the child in her arms.

Then the Cherub shut the door and said: 'I give thee now three seeds taken from that tree. When Adam is dead, place these three seeds in thy father's mouth, and bury him.'

So Seth took the seeds, and returned to his father. Adam was glad to hear what his son told him, and he praised God. On the third day after the return of Seth, he died. Then his son buried him in the skins of beasts which God had given him for a covering, and his sepulchre was on Golgotha. In course of time three trees grew from the seeds brought from Paradise: one was a cedar, another a cypress, and the third a pine. They grew with prodigious force, thrusting their boughs to right and left. It was with one of these boughs that Moses performed his miracles in Egypt, brought water out of the rock, and healed those whom the serpents slew in the desert.

After a while the three trees touched one another, then began to incorporate and confound their several natures in a single trunk. It was beneath this tree that David sat when he bewailed his sins.

In the time of Solomon this was the noblest of the trees of Lebanon. It surpassed all in the forests of King Hiram, as a monarch surpasses those who crouch at his feet. Now, when the son of David erected his palace, he cut down this tree to convert it into the main pillar supporting his roof. But all in vain. The column refused to answer this purpose. It was at one time too long, at another time too short. Surprised at this resistance, Solomon lowered the walls of his palace to suit the beam, but at once it shot up and pierced the roof, like an arrow driven through a piece of canvas, or a bird recovering its liberty. Solomon, enraged, cast the tree over Kedron, that all might trample it as they crossed the brook.

There the Queen of Sheba found it, and she, recognizing its virtue, had it raised. Solomon then buried it. Some while after, the king dug the pool of Bethseda on the spot. This pond at once acquired miraculous properties and healed the sick who flocked to it. The water owed its virtues to the beam which lay beneath it.

When the time of the Crucifixion of Christ drew nigh, this wood rose to the surface and was brought out of the water. The executioners, when seeking a suitable beam to serve for the cross, found it and made of it the instrument of the death of the Saviour. After the Crucifixion it was buried on Calvary, but it was found by the Empress Helena, mother of Constantine the Great, deep in the ground with two others on 3 May 328. Christ's cross was distinguished from those of the thieves by a sick woman being cured by touching it. This same event is, however, ascribed by a Syriac manuscript in the British Museum, unquestionably of the fifth century, to Protonice, wife of the Emperor Claudius. It was carried away by Chosroes, king of Persia, on the plundering of Jerusalem, but it was recovered by Heraclius, who defeated him in battle on the 14 September 615, a day that has ever since been commemorated as the Feast of the Exaltation of the Cross.

Such is the Legend of the Cross, one of the wildest of mediaeval fancies. It is founded, though unconsciously, on this truth: that the Cross was a sacred sign long before Christ died on it.

16.

𝔖𝔠𝔥𝔞𝔪𝔦𝔯

WHEN THE LAW was given to Moses from Sinai, Moses was told that on that spot 'There shalt thou build an altar unto the Lord thy God, an altar of stones: thou shalt not lift up any iron tool upon them.' When King Solomon erected his glorious temple, 'the house, when it was in building, was built of stone made ready before it was brought thither: so that there was neither hammer, nor axe, nor any tool of iron heard in the house while it was in building.' And the reason for the prohibition of iron in the construction of the altar is given in the Mischna – iron is used to shorten life, the altar to prolong it. The altar was the symbol of peace made between God and man, and therefore the metal employed in war was forbidden to be used in its erection. The idea was extended by Solomon to the whole temple. It is not said that iron was not used in the preparation of the building stones, but that no tool was heard in the fitting together of the parts. Around Solomon accumulated the fables which were related of the Persian heroes and adopted by the Jews as legends of native production. It was not sufficient that Solomon should have skilfully pieced together the rough stones: he was supposed to have hewn them by supernatural means, without the tool of iron.

The tale ran that as Solomon was about to build the temple without the use of iron, his wise men drew his attention to the stones of the high priest's breastplate, which had been cut and polished by something harder than themselves. This was the schamir, which was able to cut where iron would not bite. Thereupon Solomon summoned the spirits to inform him of the whereabouts of this substance. They told him schamir was a worm of the size of a barley corn, but so powerful that the hardest flint could not resist him. The spirits advised Solomon to seek Asmodeus, king of the devils, who could give him further information. When Solomon inquired where Asmodeus was to be met with, they replied that, on a distant mountain, he had dug a huge cistern out of which he daily drank. Solomon then sent Benaiah with a chain, on which was written the magic word *schem hammphorasch*, a fleece of wool and a skin of wine. Benaiah, having arrived at the cistern of Asmodeus, undermined it and let the water out by a little hole which he then plugged up with the wool; after which he filled the pit with wine. The evil spirit came, as was his wont, to the cistern and scented the wine. Suspecting treachery, he refused to drink and retired. But at length, impelled by thirst, he drank, and became intoxicated, and was promptly chained by Benaiah and carried away. Benaiah had no willing prisoner to conduct. Asmodeus plunged and kicked, upsetting trees and houses. In this manner he came near a hut in which lived a widow, and when she besought him not to injure her poor little cot, he turned aside, and in so doing broke his leg. 'Rightly,' said the devil, 'is it written "A soft tongue breaketh the bone." ' (*Proverbs* xxv 15.)

When in the presence of Solomon, Asmodeus was constrained to behave with greater decorum. Schamir, he told Solomon, was the property of the Prince of the Sea, and that prince entrusted no one with the mysterious worm except the moor-hen, which had taken an oath of fidelity to him. The moor-hen takes the schamir with her to the tops of mountains, splits them and injects seeds which grow and cover the naked rocks. Wherefore the bird is called the Naggar Tura, the mountain-carver. If Solomon desired to possess himself of the worm, he must find the nest of the moor-hen and cover it with a plate of glass, so that the mother bird could not get at her young without breaking the glass. She would then seek schamir for the purpose, and the worm must be obtained from her.

Accordingly Benaiah, son of Jehoida, sought the nest of the bird, and laid over it a piece of glass. When the moor-hen came, and could not reach her young, she flew away and fetched schamir, and placed it on the glass. Then Benaiah shouted and so terrified the bird that she dropped the worm and flew away. Benaiah by this means obtained possession of the coveted schamir, and bore it to Solomon. But the moor-hen was so distressed at having broken her oath to the Prince of the Sea that she slew herself.

According to another version Solomon went to his fountain, where he found the daemon Sackar, whom he captured by a ruse and chained down. Solomon pressed his ring to the chains, and Sackar uttered a cry so shrill that the earth quaked.

Quoth Solomon: 'Fear not; I shall restore you to liberty if you will tell me how to burrow noiselessly after minerals and metals.'

'I know not how to do so,' answered the Jin. 'But the raven can tell you. Place over her eggs a sheet of crystal and you shall see how the mother will break it.'

Solomon did so, and the mother brought a stone and shattered the crystal. 'Whence got you that stone?' asked Solomon. 'It is the stone Samur,' answered the raven. 'It comes from a desert in the uttermost east.' So the monarch sent some giants to follow the raven, and bring him a suitable number of stones.

According to a third version the bird is an eagle, and schamir is the Stone of Wisdom. Possessed of this schamir, Solomon wrought the stones for his temple.

Rabbinical fantasy has developed other myths concerning this mysterious force resident in worm or stone. On the second day of Creation were created the well by which Jacob met Rebecca, the manna which fed the Israelites, the wonder-working rod of Moses, the ass which spake to Balaam, and schamir, the means whereby without iron tool Solomon was to build the House of God. Schamir is not in early rabbinical fable a worm; the treatise Sota gives the first indication of its being regarded as something more than a stone by terming it 'a creature'. 'Our Rabbis have taught us that schamir is a creature as big as a barley-corn, created in the hexameron [*first six days of the world*] and that nothing can resist it. How is it preserved? It is wrapped in a wisp of wool and kept in a leaden box of small grains like barley-meal.' (Sota, xlviii, 8.) After the building of the temple, schamir vanished.

17.

The Piper of Hameln

HAMELN TOWN was infested with rats in the year 1284. In their houses the people had no peace from them. Rats disturbed them by night and worried them by day. One day there came a man into the town, most quaintly attired in a parti-coloured suit, and he was called Bunting, after his dress, though no one knew whence he came or who he was. He announced himself to be a rat-catcher, and offered for a certain sum of money to rid the place of vermin. The townsmen agreed to his proposal and promised him the sum demanded. Thereupon the man drew forth a pipe, and piped so that the rats swarmed to follow him out of the town as far as the river Weser, into which they all plunged and drowned. No sooner were the townsfolk released from their torment than they repented of their bargain, and on the plea that the rat-destroyer was a sorcerer they refused to pay him his fee. At this the piper angrily vowed vengeance. On 26 June, the feast of St John and St Paul, he reappeared in Hameln town. He piped, and all the children ran after him, whilst the Hameln people stood aghast, not knowing what step to take or what would be the result of this weird piping. He led the children from the town towards a hill rising above the Weser. What seemed to be a door opened in the side of the mountain, and the piper went in followed by all the children.

When all but two stragglers had gone into the mountain, the door in the cliff shut fast. Of the two who were left, one child was dumb and the other blind. The number of children who perished was one hundred and thirty. Fathers and mothers rushed to the east gate, but when they came to the Koppenberg mountain there was no sign of any gate, except a small hollow where the children had gone in. Until well into the nineteenth century two moss-grown crosses marked the spot where the children had vanished. Gold painted signs and inscriptions on wood and stone recorded the event, and for a long time, so profound was the impression produced by the event, that the town dated its public documents from this calamity of 1284.

Similar stories are told of other places: of a fiddler who did the same to the children of Brandenburg, a piper at Lorch, on the Rhine, a bagpiper in the Hartz mountains. It is singular that a parallel story should exist in Abyssinia. It is related by Harrison in his *Highlands of Ethiopia* that the Hadjiuji Madjuji are daemon pipers who, riding on a goat, irresistibly draw the children after them to destruction.

Akin to the story of the piper is that made familiar by Goethe's poem, the Erlking:

A father is riding late at night with his child wrapped in a mantle. The little fellow hears the erlking chanting in his ear, and promising him the glories of Elf-land, where his daughters dance and sing, awaiting him, if he will follow. The father hushes the child and bids him not to listen, for it is only the whistling of the wind among the trees. But the song has lured the little soul away, and when the father unfolds his mantle the child is dead.

It is curious that a trace of this myth should remain among the Wesleyans. From my experience of English dissenters, I am satisfied that their religion is, to a greater extent than any one has supposed, a revival of ancient paganism, which has long lain dormant among the English peasantry [!!]. A Wesleyan told me one day that he was sure his little servant-girl was going to die; for the night before, as he had lain awake, he had heard an angel piping at her in the adjoining room; the music was inexpressibly sweet, like the warbling of a flute. 'And when t'aingels gang that road,' said the Yorkshire man, 'they're boun to tak bairns' souls wi' em.' I know several cases of Wesleyans declaring that they were going to die, because they had heard voices singing to them, which none but themselves had distinguished, telling them of the 'happy land, far, far away,' precisely as the piper of Hameln's notes seemed to speak of a land

> Where flowers put forth a fairer hue,
> And every thing was strange and new.

And I have heard of a death being accounted for by a band of music playing in the neighbourhood. 'When t'music was agaite, her soul was forced to be off.'

A hymn by Dr Faber, now very popular, is unquestionably founded on this ancient superstition, and is probably a revival, an unconcious revival, of early dissenting reminiscences:

> Hark! hark, my soul! Angelic songs are swelling
> O'er earth's green fields and ocean's wave-beat shore;
> How sweet the truth those blessed strains are telling
> Of that new life when sin shall be no more!
>
> Onwards we go, for still we hear them singing,
> Come, weary souls, for Jesus bids you come;
> And through the dark, its echoes sweetly ringing,
> The music of the Gospel leads us home.
>   Angels of Jesus, Angels of Light,
>   Singing to welcome the pilgrims of the night.

The music which our English dissenters consider as that of angels' singing is attributed by the Germans to the Elves, and their song is called Alpleich or Elfenreigen. Children are cautioned not to listen to it, or believe in the promises made in the weird spirit-song. If they hearken, then Frau Holle, the ancient goddess Hulda, takes them to wander with her in the forests.

These northern myths resemble the classic fable of the Sirens with their magic lay – Ulysses with his ears open, bound to the mast, longing to rush to their arms and perish.

The root of the myth is this: the piper is no other than the wind, and ancients held that in the wind were the souls of the dead. The very names given to the soul, *animus*, *spiritus*, *athem*, signify wind or breath and point to the connection which was supposed to exist between them. Our word *ghost*, the German *Geist*, is from a root *gisan*, to gush and blow, as does the wind. All over England the peasants still believe that the spirits of unbaptized children wander in the wind, and that the wail at their doors and windows are the cries of the little souls condemned to journey till the last day. The ancient German goddess Hulda was ever accompanied by a crowd of children's souls, and Odin in his wild hunt rushed over the tree-tops accompanied by the scudding train of brave men's spirits. It is because the soul is thought to travel on the wind that we open the window to let a dying person breathe his last. Often I have had it repeated to me that the person *in extremis* could not die, that he struggled to die, but was unable till the casement was thrown open, and then at once his spirit escaped.

In one of the Icelandic sagas we have a strange story of a man standing at his house-door and seeing the souls go by in the air, and among the souls was his own. He told the tale, and died.

18.

𝕭𝖎𝖘𝖍𝖔𝖕 𝕳𝖆𝖙𝖙𝖔

OPPOSITE KAUB IN a reach of the river Rhine which is one of the areas most heavily frequented by tourists there is a fortified rock in midstream called the Mäusethurm, or Mouse-tower, from which visitors come away primed with the legend of God's judgment on the wicked Bishop Hatto within that very tower.

Hatto lived toward the end of the tenth century, being abbot of Fulda, farther down the Rhine, for twelve years and subsequently Bishop of Mainz. In the year 970 Germany suffered from famine. As the rhymed version of the legend goes:

> Every day the starving poor
> Crowded around Bishop Hatto's door,
> For he had a plentiful last year's store;
> And all the neighbourhood could tell
> His granaries were furnished well.

Wearied by the cries of the famishing people, the Bishop appointed a day on which he undertook to quiet them. He instructed all who were without bread or the means to buy it at the high price it was fetching then to converge on his great barn. From all quarters, far and near, the poor hungry folk flocked into Kaub, and were admitted into the barn till it could not hold any more people.

> Then, when he saw it could hold no more,
> Bishop Hatto made fast the door,

And while for mercy on Christ they call,
He set fire to the barn, and burnt them all.

'I'faith, 'tis an excellent bonfire!' quoth he,
'And the country is greatly obliged to me
For ridding it in these times forlorn
Of rats that only consume the corn.'

So then to his palace returned he,
And he sat down to supper merrily,
And he slept the night like an innocent man;
But Bishop Hatto never slept again.

For when he rose in the morning and went into his hall he found that rats had eaten his portrait out of its frame. Then a farm servant reported to him that rats had devoured all the corn in his granaries. He was followed by a messenger reporting that a legion of rats was making its way to his palace. The Bishop looked from his window and saw the roads and fields dark with the advancing army, chewing remorselessly through both hedge and wall as they made straight for his palace. Full of terror, the prelate escaped through his postern and was rowed out to his tower in the river, where he barred every entrance.

But the rats followed him, swam the river, clambered up the rock, and crawled to the slits and embrasures of the battlements. They chewed their way in by the thousand through stone wall and plank floor and ceiling, advancing towards the Bishop. In one attack, the climbed, dropped, and leapt at him from all sides:

They have whetted their teeth against the stones,
And now they pick the Bishop's bones;
They gnawed the flesh from every limb,
For they were sent to do judgment on him.

It is a relief to know that popular fiction maligned Bishop Hatto, who was not by any means a hard-hearted and wicked prelate. Wolfius, who told the story in 1600 on the authority of Marianus Scotus who died in 1086, a hundred and sixteen years after the alleged event, and of Honorius Augustodunensis who died in 1152, justified the tale by the fact that the tower still stood with its name referring to the rats. But there is documentary proof that the tower was erected as a station for collecting tolls on vessels passing up and down the river. The same story is told of other people in other places, including a Bishop of Strasburg who died only 27 years after Hatto and a Bishop of Cologne who died in 1112. Exactly the same detailed story is told of the death of the Freiherr von Güttingen, on Lake Constance, of a mouse-tower at Holözster in Austria, and of the mouse-lake Wörthsee in Bavaria and a Mäuseschloss in the Hirschberger lake. The Poles have a story, initiated by Martinus Gallus in 1110 but more fully related by Majolus (*Dierum Canic.*, p. 793), of King Popiel, a corrupt governor, who summoned dissidents to his palace and then poisoned them and flung their corpses into Lake Gopolo. He held a banquet to celebrate his new freedom from these trouble-makers, but during the feast an enormous number of mice issued from the bodies of his poisoned subjects, rushed on the palace and attacked the king and his family. Popiel took refuge within a circle of fire, but the mice broke through the flaming ring. Then he fled with his wife and child to a castle in the sea, but was followed and devoured. There is a similar Scandinavian legend. William of Malmesbury (Book iii, Bohn's translation, p. 313) tells of Henry IV of Germany, another evil monarch, who was attacked by mice, fled to sea, but was pursued by the rodents who holed the vessel and finally devoured the king.

I believe the origin of these stories of kings and nobles being eaten by vermin lies in the heathen human sacrifice made in times of famine. That such sacrifice took place among the Scandinavian and Teutonic peoples is certain. Tacitus records that the Germans sacrificed men. Snorro Sturlesson (died 1241) gives an instance of the Swedes offering their king to obtain abundant crops (Snorro Sturlesson, *Heimskringla*, Saga 1, c. 18, 47.):

Donald took the heritage after his father Visbur, and ruled over the land. As in his time there was a great famine and distress, the Swedes made great offerings of sacrifice at Upsala. The first autumn they sacrificed oxen, but the succeeding season was not improved by it. The following autumn they sacrificed men, but the succeeding year was rather worse. The third year, when the offer of sacrifices should begin, a great multitude of Swedes came to Upsala; and now the chiefs held consultations with each other, and all agreed that the times of scarcity were on account of their king Donald, and they resolved to offer him for good seasons, and to assault and kill him, and sprinkle the altar of the gods with his blood. And they did so.' And again, of Olaf the Tree-feller: 'There came dear times and famine, which they ascribed to their king, as the Swedes used always to reckon good or bad crops for or against their kings. The Swedes took it amiss that Olaf was sparing in his sacrifices, and believed the dear times must proceed from this cause. The Swedes therefore gathered together troops, made an expedition against King Olaf, surrounded his house and burnt him in it, giving him to Odin as a sacrifice for good crops.

Saxo Grammaticus says that in the reign of King Snio of Denmark there was a famine. The *Chronicon Regum Danicorum* tells a curious story about this Snio being devoured by vermin, sent to destroy him by his former master the giant Lae. Probably Snio was sacrificed, like Donald and Olaf, to obtain good harvests. It seems likely to me that the manner in which an offering for plenty was made was by exposure to rats, just as M. Du Taillu reports that an African tribe place their criminals in the way of ants to be devoured by them. Offerings to rats and mice are still prevalent among the peasantry in certain parts of Germany, if we may credit Grimm and Wolff, and this can only be a relic of heathenism, for the significance of the act is lost. Rats and mice have generally been considered sacred animals. Among the Scandinavian and Teutonic peoples they were regarded as the souls of the dead. If I am correct in supposing that the Hatto myth points to sacrifices of chieftains and princes in times of famine, and that the manner of the offering of the sacrifice was the exposure of the victim to rats, then it is not to be wondered at that, when the reason of such a sacrifice was forgotten, the death should be accounted as a judgment of God for some crime committed by the sufferer, such as hard-heartedness, murder or sacrilege.

19.

𝔐𝔢𝔩𝔲𝔰𝔦𝔫𝔞

EMMERICK, COUNT OF POITOU, was a nobleman of great
wealth and eminent for his virtues. He had two children, a son
named Bertram and a daughter Blaniferte. In the great forest which
stretched away in all directions around the knoll on which stood the
town and castle of Poictiers lived a Count de la Forêt, related to
Emmerick but poor and with a large family. Out of compassion for
his kinsman, the Count of Poitou adopted his youngest son Raymond,
a beautiful and amiable youth, and made him his constant companion in hall and in the chase. One day the Count and his retinue
hunted a boar in the forest of Colombiers, and, distancing his
servants, Emmerick found himself alone in the depths of the wood
with Raymond. The boar had escaped. Night came on, and the two
huntsmen lost their way. They succeeded in lighting a fire, and were
warming themselves over the blaze when suddenly the boar plunged
out of the forest upon the Count. Raymond snatched a sword and
struck at the beast, but the blow glanced off and slew the Count. A
second blow lay the boar at his side. Raymond then perceived with
horror that his friend and master was dead. In despair he mounted
his horse and fled, not knowing whither he went.

Presently the boughs of the trees became less interlaced and the
trunks fewer, and, next moment, his horse crashed through the
shrubs and brought him out on a pleasant glade, white with rime and
illumined by the new moon. In the midst bubbled up a limpid

fountain and flowed away over a pebbly floor with a soothing mur-
mur. Near the fountain-head sat three maidens in glimmering white
dresses, with long waving golden hair and faces of inexpressible
beauty.

Raymond was riveted to the spot with astonishment. He believed
that he saw a vision of angels and would have prostrated himself at
their feet had not one of them advanced and stayed him. The lady
inquired the cause of his manifest terror, and the young man after a
slight hesitation told her of his dreadful misfortune. She listened with
attention, and at the conclusion of the story recommended him to
remount his horse and gallop out of the forest and return to Poictiers
as though unconcious of what had taken place. All the huntsmen had
lost themselves in the wood that day, and were returning singly at
intervals to the castle, so no suspicion would attach to him. The body
of the count would be found, and from the proximity of the dead
boar it would be concluded that he had fallen before the tusk of the
animal to which he had given its death-blow.

Relieved of his anxiety, Raymond was able to devote his attention
exclusively to the beauty of the lady who addressed him, and found
means to prolong the conversation till daybreak. He had never beheld charms equal to hers, and the susceptible heart of the youth was
completely captivated by the fair unknown. Before he left her he
obtained from her a promise to be his. She then told him to ask of
his kinsman Bertram, as a gift, so much ground around the fountain
where they had met as could be covered by a stag's hide. Upon this
ground she undertook to erect a magnificent palace. Her name, she
told him, was Melusina. She was a water-fay of great power and
wealth. She consented to be his, but on one condition: that her
Saturdays might be spent in complete seclusion upon which he
should never venture to intrude.

Raymond then left her and followed her advice to the letter.
Bertram, who succeeded his father, readily granted the land he asked
for, but was not a little vexed when he found that, by cutting the
hide into threads, Raymond had succeeded in making it into a
considerable area.

Raymond then invited the young count to his wedding, and the
marriage festivities took place with unusual splendour, in the magnificent castle erected by Melusina. On the evening of the marriage
the bride, with tears in her eyes, implored her husband on no account
to attempt an intrusion on her privacy upon Saturdays, for such an

intrusion must infallibly separate them for ever. The enamoured Raymond readily swore to observe her wishes strictly in this matter.

Melusina continued to extend the castle and strengthen its fortifications, till the like was not to be seen in all the country round. On its completion she named it after herself, Lusinia, a name which has been corrupted to Lusignan, which it bears to this day. [*The castle was destroyed in 1574 as a Huguenot retreat.*]

In course of time the Lady of Lusignan gave birth to a son who was baptized Urian. He was a strangely-shaped child. His mouth was large, his ears pendulous. One of his eyes was red, the other green. A twelvemonth later she gave birth to another son whom she called Gedes. He had a face which was scarlet. In thank-offering for his birth she erected and endowed the convent of Malliers, and as a place of residence for her child built the strong castle of Favent.

Melusina then bore a third son who was christened Gyot. He was a fine handsome child, but one of his eyes was higher up in his face than the other. For him his mother built La Rochelle. Her next son, Anthony, had long claws on his fingers and was covered with hair. The next again had but a single eye. The sixth was Geoffrey with the Tooth, so called from a boar's tusk which protruded from his jaw. Other children she had, but all were in some way disfigured and monstrous.

Years passed, and the love of Raymond for his beautiful wife never diminished. Every Saturday she left him and spent the twenty-four hours in the strictest seclusion, without her husband thinking of intruding on her privacy. The children grew up to be great heroes and illustrious warriors. One, Freimund, entered the Church and became a pious monk in the abbey of Malliers. The aged Count de la Forêt and the brothers of Raymond shared in his good fortune, and the old man spent his last years in the castle with his son, whilst the brothers were furnished with money and servants suitable to their rank.

One Saturday the old father inquired at dinner after his daughter-in-law. Raymond replied that she was not visible on Saturdays. Thereupon one of his brothers, drawing him aside, whispered that strange gossiping tales were about relative to this sabbath seclusion, and that it behoved him to inquire into it and set the minds of the people at rest. Full of wrath and anxiety, the count rushed off to the private apartments of the countess, but found them empty. One door alone was locked, and that opened into a bath. He looked through the key-hole and to his dismay beheld her in the water, her lower extremities changed into the tail of a monstrous fish or serpent.

Silently he withdrew. No word of what he had seen passed his lips. It was not loathing that filled his heart, but anguish at the thought that by his fault he must lose the beautiful wife who had been the charm and glory of his life. Some time passed by, however, and Melusina gave no token of consciousness that she had been observed during the period of her transformation. But one day news reached the castle that Geoffrey with the Tooth had attacked the monastery of Malliers and burned it, and that in the flames had perished Freimund with the abbot and a hundred monks. On hearing of this disaster, the poor father, in a paroxysm of misery, exclaimed as Melusina approached to comfort him: 'Away, odious serpent, contaminator of my honourable race!'

At these words she fainted, and Raymond, full of sorrow for having spoken thus intemperately, strove to revive her. When she came to herself again, with streaming tears she kissed and embraced him for the last time. 'O husband!' she said tenderly, 'I leave two little ones in the cradle. Look tenderly after them, bereaved of their mother. And now farewell for ever! Yet know that thou, and those who succeed thee, shall see me hover over this fair castle of Lusignan whenever a new lord is to come.' And with a long wail of agony she swept from the window, leaving the impression of her foot on the stone she last touched.

The children in arms she had left were Dietrich and Raymond. At night the nurses beheld a glimmering figure appear near the cradle of the babes, most like the vanished countess, but from her waist downwards terminating in a scaly fish-tail enamelled blue and white. At her approach the little ones extended their arms and smiled, and she took them to her breast and suckled them. But as the grey dawn stole in at the casement she vanished, and the children's cries told the nurses that their mother was gone.

Long was it believed in France that the unfortunate Melusina appeared in the air, wailing over the ramparts of Lusignan before the death of one of its lords; and that on the extinction of the family she was seen whenever a king of France was to depart this life.

The story of the love of a man for a water-sprite and of her longing for normal life is an old root-tale of Aryan folk-lore with many parallels, from Undine to Hans Christian Andersen. The tale of

Melusina became immensely popular in France and Germany and Spain, appearing in a score of books during the century 1478-1577, and this pretty account is perhaps best left to make its own effect, without a superfluity of comment.

20.

The Fortunate Isles

THE PRINCIPAL MEDIAEVAL fables about the Earthly Paradise set Eden east of Asia. The Ancients had an older tradition of a vast continent called Atlantis in the far West, where there lay asleep the god who had been governor of the universe before being deposed by his son Zeus: Kronos, guarded by the hundred-handed giant Briareus. Atlantis was to the Greeks a land of rivers and woods and soft airs, occupying in their thoughts the position assumed in Christian belief by the Earthly Paradise. The Fathers of the Church waged war against this object of popular mythology, for the Scripture plainly indicated the position of the garden land as 'eastward in Eden' (*Genesis* ii 8). But in spite of their efforts to drive the western paradise from the minds of men, it held its ground and was believed in throughout the Middle Ages until Christopher Columbus sought and found Atlantis and paradise in the new world, a world in which the theories of the Ancients and of the Mediaevals met: for it was truly east of Asia and west of Europe. 'I am convinced that there [in the lands that I have discovered] is the terrestrial paradise,' Columbus wrote in 1498.

The belief in a western land, or group of islands, was prevalent among the Celts as well as the Greek and Latin geographers, and was with them an article of religion upon which were founded superstitious practices which perpetuated themselves after the introduction of Christianity.

This belief in a western land probably arose from the discovery of unfamiliar and foreign objects – canoes, timber, nuts, even occasionally bodies – which were washed up on the western coasts of Europe. (In 1508 a French vessel actually met a boat full of American Indians not far from the English coast: Bembo, *History of Venice*, vii, p. 257.) Throughout the ages this land beyond the setting sun had been called variously Meropis, the continent of Kronos, Ogygia, Atlantis, the Fortunate Isles, and the Garden of the Hesperides. These conceptions are fully analysed in Humboldt's history and geography of the New World: Humboldt, *Essai sur l'hist. de la Géographie du N. Continent*.

The Celts believed that a wall had had to be built in Britain to protect the land from the deadly influence of the other world to the west, and that the fishermen of Brittany were occupied in rowing souls across to this world. Procopius (*Ad Lycophr.* v 1200) wrote:

Beyond Gaul and nearly opposite to it, but separated by an arm of the sea, lies a ghastly region on which clouds and tempests for ever rest and which is known to its continental neighbours as the abode to which departed spirits are sent after this life. On one side of the strait dwell a few fishermen, men possessed of a very strange character and enjoying singular privileges [*i.e., freedom from taxation by the Franks*] in consideration of being the living ferrymen who, performing the office of the heathen Charon, carry the spirits of the departed to the island which is their residence after death. At the dead of night these fishermen are in rotation summoned to perform the duty by which they seem to hold permission to reside on this strange coast. A knock is heard at the door of the cottage of the man who is carrying out this singular duty. It is made by no mortal hand. A whispering, as if of a dying breeze, summons the ferryman to his duty. He hastens to his bark on the sea shore, and as soon as he has launched it he sees its hull sink perceptibly in the water in reaction to the weight of the dead with which it is filled. No form is seen, and though voices are heard the accents are undistinguishable, as of a man who talks in his sleep.

In the old romance of Lancelot du Lac the Demoiselle d'Escalot directs that after her death her body should be placed, richly adorned, in a boat and allowed to float away before the wind: a trace of the ancient belief in the passage over the sea to the land of the souls which is evident again in the *Morte d'Arthur*, that romance of a demigod who was believed in long before the birth of the historic Arthur. When the King was about to die of a mortal wound he was brought by good Sir Bedivere to the water's side:

And when they were at the water's side, even fast by the bank, hoved a little barge with many fair ladies in it, and among them all was a queen, and they all had black hoods, and they wept and shrieked when they saw King Arthur. 'Now put me into the barge,' said the king; and so he did softly; and there received him three queens with great mourning, and so these three queens set them down and in one of their laps King Arthur laid his head. And then that queen said 'Ah! dear brother, why have ye tarried so long from me? Alas! this wound on your head hath taken over-much cold.' And so then they rowed from the land, and Sir Bedivere cried 'Ah! my lord Arthur, what shall become of me now ye go from me and leave me here alone among mine enemies?' 'Comfort thyself,' said King Arthur, 'and do as well as thou mayest, for in me is no trust to trust in; for I will into the vale of Avalon for to heal me of my grievous wound: and if thou never hear more of me, pray for my soul.' But evermore the queens and the ladies wept and shrieked that it was pity for to hear them. And as soon as Sir Bedivere had lost sight of the barge, he wept and wailed, and so took to the forest.

Avalon is the Isle of the Blessed of the Celts. It is the Isle of Apples, a name reminding one of the Garden of the Hesperides in the far western seas, with its tree of golden apples in the midst. According to an ancient poem (Villemarqué, *Barz. Breiz.* i 193) it is a place of enchantment and beauty. There youths and maidens dance hand in hand on the dewy grass, and behind the woods the golden sun dips and rises. A murmuring rill flows from a spring in the middle of the island, and from it the spirits drink and obtain life with the draught. Joy, song and minstrelsy reign in that blessed realm. There all is plenty and the golden age is unending: cows give their milk in such abundance that they fill large ponds at a milking. There too is a palace of glass, floating in the air, and receiving within its transparent walls the souls of the blessed.

This distant isle, apparently so much more beautiful than para-dise, became the object of jealous satire among some mediaeval moralists, who nick-named it Cockaigne – a name referring to the good cooking found there, which seemed justified when one poet extolled it as a place where 'the birds are merrily singing, ready roasted and flying into hungry mouths . . . All down the streets go roasted geese, turning themselves; there is a river of wine; the ladies are all beautiful; new clothes are provided every month. A fountain of eternal youth bubbles up, restoring bloom and vigour to all who bathe in it, be they ever so old and ugly.' This mysterious Western

Land is in fact called in Irish Thierna na oge, the Country of Youth. The Norsemen called it Greater Ireland. The Portuguese and the Icelanders and the Gaels recited fables about it.

There in the Fortunate Isles, the Celts believed, in radiant halls dwelt the spirits of the departed, ever blooming and beautiful, ever laughing and gay. It is curious how retentive of ancient mythological doctrines about death are the memories of the people. This Celtic fable of the Land Beyond the Sea to which souls are borne after death has engrafted itself upon popular religion in England. A Sunday School Union hymn asks:

> Shall we meet beyond the river,
>   Where the surges cease to roll,
> Where in all the bright For-ever
>   Sorrow ne'er shall press the soul?
>
> Shall we meet in that blest harbour
>   When our stormy voyage is o'er?
> Shall we meet and cast the anchor
>   By the fair celestial shore?
>
> Shall we meet with many loved ones
>   Who were torn from our embrace?
> Shall we listen to their voices
>   And behold them face to face?

The popular belief in the transmigration of the soul to bliss immediately after its departure from the body is a venerable Aryan myth, but it is not Christian. The Church has consistently preached the resurrection of the body. But the doctrine of the soul being transported to heaven, and of happiness being completed at death, finds no place in the Bible, or the Liturgies of any branch – Greek, Roman or Anglican – of the Church Catholic. Yet this was the tenet of our Celtic forefathers, and it has maintained itself in English Protestantism, so as to divest the doctrine of the resurrection of the body of its grasp on the popular mind.

21.
Swan Maidens

I REMEMBER A LONG SCRAMBLE in Iceland, over the ruins of tuff rock in a narrow gorge. My little pony had toiled sturdily up the dusty slope leading apparently to nothing, when all at once the ravine terminated in an abrupt scarp, from which was obtained a sudden peep of entrancing beauty. Far away in front gleamed a snowy dome of silver resting on a base of gentian blue. To the left started sheer precipices of ink-black rock to icy pinnacles from which fell a continuous powder of white water into a lake – here black as the rocks above it, yonder bluer than the over-arching heavens. Not a sound of animated life broke the stillness, only the patter of the falling streams. The only living objects visible were two white swans rippling proudly through the clear water.

I have never since felt surprise at superstition attaching itself to these glorious birds, haunting lone tarns, pure as new-driven snow. The first night I slept under my tent in the same island I was wakened with a start by a wild triumphant strain as of clarions pealing from the sky. I crept from under the canvas to look up, and saw a flight of the Hooper swans on their way to the lakes of the interior, high up, lit by the sun, like flakes of gold-leaf against the green sky of an arctic night.

Its solitary habits, the purity of its feathers, its wondrous song, have given to the wild swan a charm which has endeared it to poets and ensured its introduction into mythology. The ancient Indians, looking up at the sky over which coursed the white cirrus clouds, made a fable about a heavenly lake in which bathed the swan-like Apsaras, impersonifications of these delicate light cloud-flakes. What these white vapours were, the ancient Aryans could not understand. Therefore, because they bore a more or less remote resemblance to swans floating on blue waters, they supposed them to be divine beings partaking of the nature and appearance of these beautiful birds. Apsaras skim as swans over the lotus-pond of heaven or, laying aside their feather-dresses, bathe as beautiful females in the limpid flood. These swan-maidens are the houris of the Vedic heaven, receiving to their arms the souls of heroes. Sometimes they descend to earth and become the wives of mortals. But soon their celestial nature re-asserts itself, and they expand their luminous wings and soar away into the heavenly deeps of tranquil azure.

There are folk-tales of swan-maidens in earliest Sanskrit. The Samoyeds [*Siberian Mongols*] have a traditional story of a particularly wild adventure with swan-maidens: Two Samoyeds lived on a desolate steppe where they caught foxes, sables and bears. One went on a journey and passed an old woman chopping birch-trees. He cut down the trees for her and dragged them to her tent. In gratitude the old woman told him to hide and see what would take place. He did so, and soon saw seven maidens approach. They asked the old woman whether she had cut the wood herself and whether she was quite alone, and she said Yes to both questions. They went away. The old woman called to the Samoyed and told him to follow the damsels and steal the dress of one of them. He obeyed. Emerging from a wood of gloomy pines, he came upon a beautiful lake in which the seven maidens were swimming. He took away the dress which lay nearest to him. The seven swam to the shore and sought their clothes. Those of one were gone. She cried bitterly and exclaimed: 'I will be the wife of the man who stole my dress if he will give it back.' He replied 'No, I will not give you back your feather dress, or you will spread your wings and fly away from me.' 'Give me my clothes, I am freezing.' 'Not far from here,' said the man, 'there are seven Samoyeds who range the neighbourhood by day, and at night hang their hearts on the tent-pegs. Get me those hearts, and I will give you your clothes.' 'In five days I will bring them to you,' said the maiden, so the man gave her her clothes and returned to his companion.

One day the maiden came out of the sky and asked him to accompany her to the brothers whose hearts he had set her to obtain. They came to the tent. The man hid but the damsel became invisible. At night the seven Samoyeds returned, ate their supper, and then hitched up their hearts to the tent-pegs. The swan-maiden stole them and brought them to her lover. He dashed all but one to the ground, and as they fell, the brothers died. But the heart of the eldest he did not kill. Then the man without a heart awoke and begged to have it returned to him.

'Once upon a time you killed my mother,', said the Samoyed. 'Restore her to life and you shall have your heart.'

Then the man without a heart said to his wife 'Go to the place where the dead lie. There you will find a purse. In that purse is her soul. Shake the purse over the dead woman's bones, and she will come to life.' The woman did as she was ordered, and the mother of the Samoyed came to life. Then he dashed the heart to the ground, and the last of the seven brothers died.

But the swan-maiden took her own heart and that of her husband, and threw them into the air. The mother of the Samoyed saw that they were without hearts, so she went to the lake where the six maidens were swimming. She stole one dress, and would not give it back until the maiden had promised to recover the hearts that were in the air. This was done, the lovers were cherishing their hearts, and the swan-maiden got her dress back again.

In the swan-myths of classical Greece the swan was the bird of the Muses, and therefore also of Apollo. When that golden-haired deity was born, swans came from the golden stream of Pactolus and wheeled around the island of Delos seven times, sounding songs of joy.

In the fable of Leda, Zeus – the heaven above – clothed in swan's shape – that is, enveloped in white mist – embraces the fair Leda, who is probably the earth-mother, and by her becomes the father of the Dioscuri, the morning and evening twilights; and, according to some, he becomes also the father of beautiful Helen, that is, Selene, the moon.

An old German story tells of a nobleman who was hunting in a forest when he came out upon a lake in which an exquisitely beautiful maiden was bathing. He stole up to her and took from her the gold necklace she wore. Then she lost her power to fly, and she became his wife. At one birth she bore seven sons, who had all of them gold chains round their necks, and had the power, which their mother had possessed, of transforming themselves into swans at pleasure.

In the ancient Gudrun-lied an angel approaches like a swimming wild-bird. It is a fair subject for inquiry, whether the popular iconography of the angel-hosts is not indebted to the heathen myth for its most striking features. Our delineations of angels in flowing white robes, with large pinions, are derived from the later Greek and Roman representations of victory. But were not these figures – half bird, half woman – derived from the Apsaras of the Vedas, who were but the fleecy clouds, supposed in the ages of Man's simplicity to be celestial swans?

22.

The Knight of the Swan

THE EARLY ENGLISH romance of Helias, the Knight of the Swan, was ostensibly a popular pedigree giving a mystic ancestry to Godfrey of Bouillon, the leader of the first Crusade, who paid homage to the Emperor at Constantinople in 1097, marched to Jerusalem two years later, and became King of Jerusalem for the remaining year before he died at the age of 40 in 1100. The romance incorporates the myth of the Knight of the Swan, which was as popular in folk-lore as Godfrey of Bouillon was as a people's hero, and it is of course told of Lohengrin. The English version starts: 'We rede in the auncient and autentike cronykills that sometime ther was a noble king in Lilefort [*i.e.*, *L'Île Fort*] otherwise named the strong yle, a muche riche lande, the which kinge had to name Pieron. And he took to wife and spouse Matabrunne the doughter of an other king puissaunt and riche mervailously . . .' But the quaintness of early English spelling is an effect that can be over-valued, and the story will be continued more legibly:

King Pieron and Matabrune had a son, Oriant, who reigned when his father died, living in the palace with his widowed mother Matabrune. One day, hunting in the forest, King Oriant lost his way, and while resting by a fountain met a party comprising a young damsel of a noble but sad demeanour escorted by a knight with two squires and supported by three ladies in waiting. Oriant eventually married this lady, Beatrice, much to the dismay and enmity of his mother

Matabrune, who was displaced in the palace. Shortly afterwards, Oriant was called away to war, and he entrusted Beatrice to Matabrune. The time came for the pregnant Beatrice to be delivered, and her false mother-in-law prepared a wicked plan. 'Suddenly in great pain and travail of body Beatrice childed six sons and a fair daughter, at whose birth each of them brought a chain of silver about their necks issuing out of their mother's womb. And when Matabrune saw the seven children born each having a chain of silver at the neck, she had them secretly taken aside by a chambermaid under her influence and then took seven little dogs that she had prepared, and laid them all bloody under the queen as if they had issued from her body.'

Matabrune ordered her squire to drown the seven children in the river, but in compassion he left them in the forest in his cloak, where a hermit found them and nurtured them and baptized them, calling the most beautiful of the boys Helias. One day these children were seen in the forest, all with silver chains round their necks, by a servant of Matabrune who reported it immediately to the queen-mother, and she again gave orders for the children to be slaughtered. But the hired assassins found only six children – the hermit having taken Helias on a begging excursion – and they spared the infants, only robbing them of their silver chains. 'Now as soon as their chains were off, they were all changed in an instant to fair white swans by the divine grace, and they began to fly in the air over the forest making a piteous and lamentable cry.'

Helias grew up with his godfather in the forest. The hermit was told by an angel in a vision whose children these were. At the palace eventually Matabrune's campaign of malice against Beatrice was succeeding and a false charge was brought against the queen. But Helias was by now a young man, and as Beatrice was about to be executed he appeared in the lists, and by his valour proclaimed her innocence and confounded Matabrune.

Helias, reunited with his father, asked for the silver chains that had been taken from his brothers and sister, and swore that he would never rest until he had found the swans and returned to them their chains. He did come across them, and they recognised him, 'and came lightly fawning and flickering about him making him cheer.' To five of them Helias restored the chains and they returned to their human form. But the sixth chain had been melted to make a silver goblet, and one of the brothers was unable to regain human shape.

One day in L'Île Fort Helias saw this swan, his brother, guiding in a ship to the wharf, and he took it as a sign 'that I ought to go by the guiding of the swan into some country for to have honour and consolation.' He took ceremonial leave of his family and sailed away. At this time Otho, Emperor of Germany, held court at Neumagen to decide a claim by the Count of Frankfort for the duchy of Bouillon, then held by Clarissa as Duchess of Bouillon. The right was to be decided by single combat, and Duchess Clarissa had to find a champion to fight the Count of Frankfort. God sent Helias's ship sailing up the Meuse at this time, led by a swan who drew the craft by a silver chain. Helias championed Clarissa, won the battle, married her and became the Duke of Bouillon. Before the marriage he had warned the lady that if she asked his name he would have to leave her. Clarissa had a number of children including Godfrey de Bouillon, later King of Jerusalem. One night she forgot her husband's warning and began to ask him about his name and kindred. Then he rebuked her sorrowfully and, leaving his bed, bade her farewell. Instantly the swan re-appeared on the river, drawing the little boat after it, and uttering loud cries to call its brother. Helias stepped into the boat, and the swan swam with it out of the sight of the sorrowing lady.

This fable is a very ancient and popular myth, told in many cultures and about many heroes, sometimes of Lohengrin or Gerhard the Swan, whilst the lady is sometimes Beatrice of Cleves or Else of Brabant. In the twelfth century it became localized about the Lower Rhine. It is a compilation of at least two distinct myths, one about the Swan-children, the other of the Swan-knight. The home of the fable was that borderland where Germans and Celts met, where the Nibelungen legends were brought in contact with the romances of Arthur and the Sangreal.

Lohengrin belongs to the Round Table. The hero who releases Beatrice of Cleves is called Elias Grail. Pighius (*Hercules Prodicus*, Colon., 1609) related that in ancient annals Elias came from the blessed land of the earthly paradise which is called Graele. The name Elias is a corruption of the Celtic for 'swan'. I believe the story of the Knight of the Swan to be a myth of local Brabantine origin. Hence the story of Lohengrin:

The Duke of Limburg and Brabant died leaving as an only daughter Else, and committing her to the care of a brave knight Frederick von Telramund. But after the duke's death Frederick claimed the hand of Else, and the Emperor Henry the Fowler gave permission for the issue to be decided by single combat. Else sought in vain for a champion.

Then, far away in the sacred temple of the Grail at Montsalvatsch, the bell tolled untouched by human hands, a signal that help was needed. At once Lohengrin, son of Percival was sent to the rescue but he did not know where to go. As he stood foot in stirrup, ready to mount, a swan appeared on the river drawing a ship. Lohengrin abandoned his horse and embarked on a five-day journey, and only at the hour when the lists opened did Else perceive the arrival of the boat drawn by the silver swan, with Lohengrin in it, asleep on his shield. Lohengrin championed Else, and the knight of the Grail won the fight and took Else and her duchy. But he insisted that she should never ask his race. One day in a tournament he overthrew the Duke of Cleves and broke his arm, at which the Duchess of Cleves exclaimed: 'This Lohengrin may be a strong man and a Christian, but who knows whence he has sprung!' These words reached the Duchess of Brabant, and troubled her, and as she sobbed in bed Lohengrin asked her what ailed her. At first she merely replied 'The Duchess of Cleves has wounded me.' After nights of sobbing, she was provoked to plead: 'Husband, be not angry, but I must know whence you have sprung.'

Then Lohengrin told her that his father was Percival and that God had sent him from the custody of the Grail. And he called his children to him and kissed them and said: 'Here are my horn and my sword. Keep them carefully; and here, my wife, is my ring which my mother gave me. Never part with it.' And at break of day the swan reappeared on the river, drawing the little shallop. Lohengrin reentered the boat, and departed never to return.

The myth is a Belgic religious myth. Just as in the Celtic legends of the Fortunate Isles we hear of mortals who went by ship to Avalon, the land of the spirits, and then returned to their fellow-mortals, so in this Belgic fable we have a denizen of the distant paradise coming by boat to this inhabited land, and leaving it again.

23.

The Sangreal

WHEN SIR LANCELOT came to the palace of King Pelles, in the words of Sir Thomas Malory in the *Mort d'Arthur*,

. . . either of them made much of each other, and so they went into the castle for to take their repast. And anon there came in a dove at the window, and in her bill there seemed a little sencer [*censer*] of gold, and therewith was such a savour as though all the spicery of the world had been there; and forthwith all there was upon the table all manner of meates and drinkes that they could thinke upon. So there came a damosell, passing faire and young, and she beare a vessell of gold betweene her hands, and thereto the king kneeled devoutly and said his prayers, and so did all that were there: 'Oh, Jesu!' said Sir Launcelot, 'what may this meane?' 'This is,' said King Pelles, 'the richest thing that any man hath living; and when this thing goeth about, the round-table shall be broken. And wit ye well,' said King Pelles, 'that this is the holy Sangreall which ye have heere seene.'

The next to see the sacred vessel was the pious Sir Bors. Then, one day while King Arthur and his court were at Camelot sitting at supper,

Anon they heard cracking and crying of thunder, that hem thought the place should all to-rive; in the midst of the blast entred a sunne-beame more clear by seaven times than ever they saw day, and all they were alighted by the grace of the Holy Ghost. Then began every knight to behold each other, and either saw other by their seeming fairer than ever they saw afore, nor for then there was no knight that might speake any word a great while; and so they looked every man on other as though they had been dombe. Then there entred into the hall the holy grale covered with white samite, but there was none that might see it, nor beare it, and there was all the hall fulfilled with good odours, and every knight had such meate and drinke as he best loved in this world; and when the holy grale had beene borne through the hall, then the holy vessel departed suddenly, and they wist not where it became.

Then the knights stood up in their places one after another, and vowed to go in quest of the Sangreal, and not to return to the Round-Table till they had obtained a full view of it.

The history of the Grail is embodied in the romance of the San Greal, the *Perceval* of Chrétien de Troyes, written at the close of the twelfth century, and in the *Titurel and Parcival* of Wolfram von Eschenbach, translated from romances older than that of Chrétien de Troyes.

When Christ was transfixed by the spear, there flowed from His side blood and water. Joseph of Arimathaea collected the blood in the vessel from which the Saviour had eaten the last supper. The enraged Jews cast Joseph into prison, and left him to die of hunger. But for forty-two years he lay in the dungeon nourished and invigorated by the sacred vessel which was in his possession. Titus released Joseph from prison, and received baptism at his hands. Then Joseph started with the vessel and the blood, or the Sangreal, for Britain. Before he died he confided the sacred treasure to his nephew. But according to another version of the legend, the Grail was preserved in heaven, till there should appear on earth a race of heroes worthy to become its guardians. Eventually angels brought this vessel to Titurel, a Breton prince, chosen by God to found the worship of the Sangreal among the Gauls. The Grail was only visible to the baptized, and only partially if they were tainted by sin. Every Good Friday a white dove descended from heaven bearing a white oblation which it laid before the Grail. The holy vessel gave oracles, expressed miraculously in characters which appeared on the surface of the bowl and then vanished. Spiritual blessings attended on the vision and custody of the sacred vessel. The guardians, and those who were privileged to behold it, were conscious of a mysterious internal joy, a foretaste of that of heaven. The material blessings were great. The Grail stood in the place of all food, it supplied its worshippers with the meats they most desired and the drinks most to their taste. It maintained them in perpetual youth. The day on which the Grail had been seen, its guardians were incapable of being wounded or suffering any hurt. If they fought for eight days after the vision they were susceptible of wounds, but not death. The knights who watched the Grail were patterns of virtue. All sensual love, even within marriage, was strictly forbidden. A single thought of passion would obscure the eye and conceal the mystic vessel. The chief of this order of knights was entitled King. As his office was hereditary, he was permitted to marry.

When the faith, or the right, was in jeopardy, a bell rang in the chapel of the Grail, and a knight was bound to go forth sword in hand to the defence. Wherever he was, should a question be asked of him as to his condition or office in the sanctuary, he was to refuse to answer and at once to return to Montsalvatsch.

Years passed, and the last hereditary king (King Pelles in the Morte d'Arthur) lay wounded in his palace. The brotherhood of the Grail was dissolved, and the existence of the sanctuary and its mystic rites was almost forgotten. Malory makes the king's healing depend on the arrival of a knight who is a 'clean maid' who shall apply to him the sacred blood. In the fulness of time Galahad, the Good Knight, came to King Arthur's court, and went forth with the other knights to the quest of the Holy Grail.

Sir Lancelot did see the Grail, but because of his sins he was paralysed by the sight. Sir Galahad, with Sir Percival and Sir Bors beheld it in the castle of King Pelles, graced by the appearance of Joseph of Arimathaea, 'the first bishop in Christendom', and of a spear which dripped drops of blood which were collected by an angel in a box. Finally the Lord Jesus appeared, and entrusted the Sangreal to Sir Galahad.

It is very certain that Chrétien de Troyes was not the inventor of this mystic tale, for there exists in the Red Book, a volume of Welsh romances preserved in the library of Jesus College, Oxford, a Welsh tale which is indisputably the original. It was a pagan druidic mystery which was first adapted to Christinity by a British hermit, possibly living about A.D. 720, who wrote a Latin legend on the subject.

24.

𝕿𝖍𝖊𝖔𝖕𝖍𝖎𝖑𝖚𝖘

A FEW YEARS BEFORE the Persian invasion in 538 there lived in the town of Adana in Cilicia a priest named Theophilus, treasurer and archdeacon. He lived in strict observance of all his religious duties, was famous for his liberality to the poor, his sympathy with the affected and afflicted, his eloquence in the pulpit, his private devotion and his severe asceticism. On the decease of the bishop, by popular acclamation he was summoned to the episcopal oversight of the diocese, but his deep humility urged him to refuse the office, even when it was pressed upon him by the metropolitan. Seldom has a *nolo episcopari* been carried out to such an emphatic refusal as was given by Theophilus. A stranger was raised to the vacant seat, and the treasurer resumed his course of life as he had pursued it for so many years. Virtue invariably arouses the spirit of detraction, and Theophilus, by his refusal of the bishopric, was thrust into public notice and attracted public attention. The consequence was that evil-minded and envious people originated slanders which, circulating widely, produced a revulsion of feeling towards Theophilus, and, by being generally reported, were accepted as substantially true. These stories reached the ears of the new bishop, and he sent for the archdeacon, and without properly investigating the charges concluded that he was guilty and deprived him of his offices.

One would have supposed that the humility which had required the holy man to refuse a mitre would have rendered him callous to the voice of slander, and have sustained him under deprivation. But the trial was too great for his virtue. He brooded over the accusations raised against him and the wrongs inflicted upon him till the whole object of his labour was the clearing of his character. He sought every available means of unmasking the calumnies of those who had maligned him and of exposing the falsity of the charges raised against him. But he found himself unable to effect his object. One man is powerless against a multitude, and slander is a hydra which, when maimed in one head, produces others in the place of that struck off. Baffled, despairing and without a friend to sustain his cause, the poor clerk sought redress in a manner which, a month ago, would have filled him with horror. He visited a necromancer, who led him at midnight to a place where four cross-roads met, and there conjured up Satan, who promised reinstatement in all his offices if the unfortunate Theophilus, in order to obtain a complete clearing of his character, would sign away his soul with a pen dipped in his own blood, and would abjure for ever Jesus Christ and His spotless mother.

On the morrow the bishop discovered the error in his judgment and sent for Theophilus. He acknowledged publicly that he had been misled by false reports, the utter valuelessness of which he was frankly ready to admit; and he asked pardon of the priest for having unjustly deprived him of office. The populace enthusiastically reversed their late opinion of the treasurer, recognised the simple virtue of the pious man, and greeted him as their saint and their confessor. For some days all went well, and in the excitement of a return to his former occupation the compact he had made was forgotten. But after a while, as reason and religion resumed their sway, the conscience of Theophilus gave him no rest. He paced his room at nights in an agony of terror. His face lost its colour. His brow was seamed with wrinkles. An unutterable horror gleamed from his deep-set eyes. Hour by hour he prayed, but he found no relief. At length he resolved on a solemn fast of forty days. This he accomplished, praying nightly in the church of the Panhagia till the grey of morning stole in at the little windows of the dome and obscured the lamps. On the fortieth night the Blessed Virgin appeared to him and sadly rebuked him for his sin. He implored her pardon and all-prevailing intercession, and this she promised him. The following night she re-appeared and assured him that Christ had, at her prayer, forgiven him. With a cry of joy he awoke; and on his breast lay the deed which had made over his soul to Satan, obtained from the evil one by the mercy of the sacred Mother of God.

The next day was Sunday. He rose, spent some time in acts of thanksgiving, and then went to church where the divine liturgy was being celebrated. After the reading of the gospel he flung himself at the bishop's feet and requested permission to make his confession in public. Then he related the circumstances of his fall, and showed the compact signed with his blood to the assembled multitude. Having finished his confession, he prostrated himself before the bishop and asked for absolution. The deed was torn and burned before the people. He was reconciled, and received the blessed sacrament: after which he returned to his house in a fever, and died at the expiration of three days. The Church honours him as a penitent, every year on 4 February.

The original account of this famous compact with the devil is in the Greek of Eutychianus, disciple of Theophilus, who declares that he related what he had seen with his own eyes and heard from the mouth of Theophilus himself. From the Greek of Eutychianus two early Latin versions are extant, one by Paulus Duaconus, the other by Gentianus Hervetus. The former of these is published in the great work of the Bollandists, who fix the date of the event in 538. The version of Gentianus Hervetus purports to be a translation from Symeon Metaphrastes, who flourished in the tenth century, and who embodied the narrative of Eutychianus in his great collection of the *Lives of the Saints*. Many subsequent versions were made from the tenth century, and Archbishop Aelfric, who died in 1006, alludes to the story in his *Homilies*. In the cathedral of Notre Dame in Paris there are two sculptured representations of the fable.

I do not think it improbable that this famous story may rest on a foundation of truth; indeed it bears on the face of it tokens of autheticity. Theophilus is driven from his position by slanders: this preys on his mind. By some means he is reinstated. The revulsion of feeling upsets his reason. He undertakes a prodigious fast, goes crazy, tells a long rambling story about a compact with the devil, and dies three days later in a brain fever. His narrative is the only extraordinary item in the tale. If we remember that this was told after a forty-days' fast and immediately before a mortal fever, the only thing to be wondered at in the legend is that any sane persons believed his ravings to have in them a foundation of truth.

A NOTE ON THE TYPEFACE

This book was composed on the Monotype in Baskerville, Series 169, a face based upon the designs of John Baskerville (1707-75). The wide letter forms of the Dutch and English Old faces were retained in English Transitional and Modern faces, but it was Baskerville who was the first to move in the direction of vertical stress. The face's generous proportions make it one of the most handsome and legible of designs. The width of the letters counteracts the vertical pull of the stress, and the open counters and clean, crisp lines make it possible to print well on a wide variety of papers. The italic is narrower than the roman, and its design clearly shows the influence of contemporary handwriting. The Monotype cutting was undertaken in 1923.